people in the NEWS

Sonia Sotomayor

by Phyllis Raybin Emert

LUCENT BOOKS
A part of Gale, Cengage Learning

GALE
CENGAGE Learning™

Detroit • New York • San Francisco • New Haven, Conn • Waterville, Maine • London

GALE
CENGAGE Learning

This book is dedicated to Larry Emert, my rock and anchor, who has made all things possible.

And to all the good dogs: Toby, Cammy, Sarah Bear, Jenny, Gabrielle, Blondie, and Dax.

LIBRARY OF CONGRESS CATALOGING-IN-PUBLICATION DATA

Emert, Phyllis Raybin.
  Sonia Sotomayor / by Phyllis Raybin Emert.
    p. cm. -- (People in the news)
  Includes bibliographical references and index.
  ISBN 978-1-4205-0489-7 (hardcover)
  1. Sotomayor, Sonia, 1954- 2. Judges--United States--Biography. I. Title.
KF8745.S67E467 2011
347.73'2634--dc22
[B]
<div align="right">2010044936</div>

Lucent Books
27500 Drake Rd.
Farmington Hills, MI 48331

ISBN-13: 978-1-4205-0489-7
ISBN-10: 1-4205-0489-4

Printed in the United States of America
1 2 3 4 5 6 7 15 14 13 12 11

Printed by Bang Printing, Brainerd, MN, 1st Ptg., 03/2011

Contents

F ame and celebrity are alluring. People are drawn to those who walk in fame's spotlight, whether they are known for great accomplishments or for notorious deeds. The lives of the famous pique public interest and attract attention, perhaps because their experiences seem in some ways so different from, yet in other ways so similar to, our own.

Newspapers, magazines, and television regularly capitalize on this fascination with celebrity by running profiles of famous people. For example, television programs such as *Entertainment Tonight* devote all of their programming to stories about entertainment and entertainers. Magazines such as *People* fill their pages with stories of the private lives of famous people. Even newspapers, newsmagazines, and television news frequently delve into the lives of well-known personalities. Despite the number of articles and programs, few provide more than a superficial glimpse at their subjects.

Lucent's People in the News series offers young readers a deeper look into the lives of today's newsmakers, the influences that have shaped them, and the impact they have had in their fields of endeavor and on other people's lives. The subjects of the series hail from many disciplines and walks of life. They include authors, musicians, athletes, political leaders, entertainers, entrepreneurs, and others who have made a mark on modern life and who, in many cases, will continue to do so for years to come.

These biographies are more than factual chronicles. Each book emphasizes the contributions, accomplishments, or deeds that have brought fame or notoriety to the individual and shows how that person has influenced modern life. Authors portray their subjects in a realistic, unsentimental light. For example, Bill Gates—the cofounder and chief executive officer of the software giant Microsoft—has been instrumental in making personal computers the most vital tool of the modern age. Few dispute his business savvy, his perseverance, or his technical expertise, yet critics say he is ruthless in his dealings with competitors and driven more by his desire to maintain Microsoft's dominance in the computer industry than by an interest in furthering technology.

In these books, young readers will encounter inspiring stories about real people who achieved success despite enormous obstacles. Oprah Winfrey—the most powerful, most watched, and wealthiest woman on television today—spent the first six years of her life in the care of her grandparents while her unwed mother sought work and a better life elsewhere. Her adolescence was colored by pregnancy at age fourteen, rape, and sexual abuse.

Each author documents and supports his or her work with an array of primary and secondary source quotations taken from diaries, letters, speeches, and interviews. All quotes are footnoted to show readers exactly how and where biographers derive their information and provide guidance for further research. The quotations enliven the text by giving readers eyewitness views of the life and accomplishments of each person covered in the People in the News series.

In addition, each book in the series includes photographs, annotated bibliographies, timelines, and comprehensive indexes. For both the casual reader and the student researcher, the People in the News series offers insight into the lives of today's newsmakers—people who shape the way we live, work, and play in the modern age.

Pursuing the Dream

"I am an ordinary person who has been blessed with extraordinary opportunities and experiences,"[1] Judge Sonia Sotomayor remarked to President Barak Obama. It was May 26, 2009, and the President had just nominated the fifty-four-year-old New Yorker to the U.S. Supreme Court. If approved by the Senate, she would be the first Hispanic—and only the third female—Supreme Court justice in the history of the Court. But Sotomayor is no ordinary person, and her story is uniquely American.

Obama summed up her life by declaring, "She's faced down barriers, overcome the odds, lived out the American Dream that brought her parents here so long ago. And even as she has accomplished so much in her life, she has never forgotten where she began, never lost touch with the community that supported her."[2]

Hard Work and High Hopes in Childhood

Sotomayor's dreams started when she was a young girl in the South Bronx housing projects of New York City. She was the oldest child of Puerto Rican parents who came to the United States to make new lives for themselves. As a young girl, two things happened that were to forever change her life. She was diagnosed with juvenile diabetes at age eight, which she controls to this day with daily insulin injections. A year later her father died, leaving her mother as the sole support of Sonia and her younger brother Juan.

The support, hard work, encouragement, and love from her mother and extended family allowed Sotomayor to succeed beyond her expectations. She studied hard in school and did not let being poor change her dreams. She set her sights on being a lawyer and then a judge, thanks in part to the popular television program *Perry Mason* that she watched every week in the 1950s and early 1960s. She told writer Greg B. Smith of the *New York Daily News* in 1998, "I was going to college and I was going to become an attorney, and I knew that when I was 10."[3]

Sotomayor began working on weekends when she was fourteen years old to help earn money for the family. "During the school week, we had to study, but on the weekends I worked Saturdays and Sundays," she explained in a Visiones public television interview in 1997. "I worked every summer and . . . during every school year . . . and I did a thousand different things."[4]

Education and Activism

Her dedication and hard work led to graduation as the class valedictorian from Cardinal Spellman high school in 1972 and a scholarship to Princeton, one of the country's top universities. When she arrived at Princeton, she realized her English writing skills were not as good as her classmates. "I found . . . that my Latina background had created difficulties in my writing that I needed to overcome. . . . My writing was stilted

Pronounce It Correctly

The proper pronunciation of Justice Sotomayor's name puts the accent on the last syllable: Sew–Toe–May–YORE.

Sonia Sotomayor graduated summa cum laude from Princeton University in 1976.

and overly complicated, my grammar and vocabulary skills weak,"[5] declared Sotomayor in a 1996 speech at Princeton. She taught herself how to write better in English and studied hard to catch up with the other students, many of whom had attended expensive prep schools.

Sotomayor graduated from Princeton in 1976 with highest academic honors (summa cum laude) and won a scholarship to Yale Law School. She earned her law degree in 1979.

Criminal Law and Private Practice

After graduating from law school Sotomayor became an assistant district attorney in New York City. She spent five years in the trial division. She investigated cases, interviewed witnesses, and helped convict many criminals. In 1984 she switched to civil law and accepted a job in private practice as an associate attorney at the firm of Pavia & Harcourt. "I wanted to complete myself as an attorney,"[6] Sotomayor later told the *New York Daily News*. She dealt with numerous international clients who had business interests in the United States and was made a partner in the firm in 1988. In the course of her work, Sotomayor met many notable people and became known as an excellent, hardworking attorney.

Dreams Become Reality

When a position on the U.S. District Court became available in 1991, U.S. senator Daniel Patrick Moynihan (D-NY) wanted to appoint a Hispanic judge from New York. His staff recommended Sotomayor. Moynihan submitted her name, and President George H.W. Bush nominated her on November 27, 1992. She was confirmed unanimously by the U.S. Senate on August 11 as judge for the U.S. District Court for the Southern District of New York. Not only was Sotomayor the first Hispanic judge in the Empire State, she was also the youngest at thirty-eight. But her sights were set on even higher accomplishments.

In 1997 President Bill Clinton nominated Sotomayor to the U.S. Court of Appeals for the Second Circuit. The Republicans in the Senate believed she was on the fast track to the Supreme Court and purposely slowed the nomination process. She was finally confirmed more than a year later, on October 7, 1998. The Republicans' suspicions that Sotomayor was destined for the Supreme Court were correct, but that achievement took eleven more years.

Sotomayor made history after the Senate confirmed her nomination to the Supreme Court by a vote of 68-31 on August 6,

You Say Hispanic, I Say Latina

Supreme Court justice Sonia Sotomayor has always referred to herself as "a Latina judge." But the media and even President Obama use the word "Hispanic." *Slate* political reporter Christopher Beam writes that "Hispanic is an English word that originally referred to people from Spain and eventually expanded to include the populations of its colonies in South and Central America." He explains that *Latino* is a Spanish word, and the feminine form is *Latina*. It usually refers to those with their roots in Latin America, not Spain.

Beam notes that the word *Hispanic* was not used until the 1980 census. In 1997 the Office of Management and Budget, which conducts the census, changed the category to "Hispanic or Latino." The Census Bureau put both terms together as one category defined as "persons who trace their origin or descent to Mexico, Puerto Rico, Cuba, Spanish-speaking Central and South American countries, and other Spanish cultures."

Ultimately, which term to use is a personal choice, and Sotomayor prefers the Spanish *Latina*.

Christopher Beam, "Is Hispanic the Same Thing as Latina?" *Slate*, May 27, 2009. www .slate.com/toolbar.aspx?action=print&id=2219165.

2009. She was sworn in officially by Chief Justice John G. Roberts Jr. on August 8, 2009. Justice Sotomayor has more than thirty years' experience in every aspect of the law. According to a White House press release, that is "more federal judicial experience to the Supreme Court than any justice in 100 years, and more overall judicial experience than anyone confirmed for the Court in the past 70 years."[7]

The dream came true for the ten-year-old from the projects. But it took years of hard work, education, sacrifice, and commitment to the law. She may have accomplished her ultimate goal, becoming an associate justice on the highest court in the land, but the job is just beginning. Supreme Court justices are appointed for life and serve until they die, retire, resign, or if they are convicted of a crime. Sotomayor may be interpreting the law and making important decisions for the next twenty to thirty years.

Chapter 1

The Early Years: Overcoming Adversity

S onia Sotomayor's childhood was not an easy one. Born to a poor family on June 25, 1954, Sonia's parents worked hard to support her and her brother Juan. But the Sotomayors were rich in another way. The writer Jonah Winter says it best in his book *A Judge Grows in the Bronx*. He writes, "Sonia's family surrounded her like a warm blanket."[8] She had plenty of love, comfort, and support in her early years, and she needed that to get her through the difficult times ahead.

The Commonwealth of Puerto Rico

"Like many other immigrants to this great land," said Sotomayor in a 2001 speech at the UC Berkeley School of Law, "my parents came [to America] because of poverty and to attempt to find and secure a better life for themselves and the family that they hoped to have."[9] Her mother, Celina Baez, was born in 1927 in the rural Santa Rosa neighborhood of Lajas on Puerto Rico's southwest coast, west of San Juan. Her father Juan Sotomayor (born ca. 1921), came from the Santurce area of San Juan.

The Baez family lived in poverty. Celina and her four brothers and sisters had only one pencil to share at school. Her parents watched over the pencil and let each child take turns using it. Most people in Puerto Rico were illiterate (about 60 percent), but Celina loved school and memorized all her lessons.

Celina's mother was ill and bedridden for years and died when Celina was nine. Then her father deserted the family, and she was raised by an older sister. Celina found a way out of Puerto Rico by enlisting in the Women's Army Corps (the WACs) in World War II when she was seventeen years old. The commonwealth of Puerto Rico is an unincorporated American territory (not a state), and those who move to the United States are considered citizens.

Sotomayor was born to a poor family on June 25, 1954. Her mother Celina and father Juan came to America to escape poverty.

Coming to America

Celina was sent to Georgia in 1944 to train as a telephone operator. After her army service, she moved to the Bronx and met her husband Juan, who had also moved from Puerto Rico. They were soon married. Juan got a job as a tool-and-die worker in a factory, while Celina got her high school equivalency diploma.

Armed with a high school education and some fluency in English, Celina found work as a switchboard operator at a small private medical facility in the Bronx called Prospect Hospital.

Sotomayor with her mother Celina in 2009. Celina got a nursing degree and worked at the Bronx Prospect Hospital.

In a speech she made in 2007, when she was inducted to the Wall of Fame of a Bronx Community Health Center, Sotomayor related a story of her mother's early experiences at the hospital. "The hospital [staff] for my entire childhood would tell me the story of when Mommy got on the loudspeaker, on the intercom to page people," the future judge related. "Once a day she had to tell the nurses to come down and bring their sheets down. . . . She couldn't say the word sheets [because of her accent]." Sotomayor laughed, "They had to take her off the switchboard for obvious reasons."[10]

Celina continued to work many years for Prospect Hospital. She started on the switchboard, then studied and got a practical nursing degree. Sotomayor remembers the hospital staff fondly. "I knew from the example of these people," she said, "that if I worked hard, if I studied, but more importantly, if I cared, I could succeed beyond my wildest dreams."[11]

Moving Up

Today, when people think of housing projects, they often think of poverty, gangs and drugs, and graffiti-marred corridors with broken elevators. It was different in 1957, when the Sotomayors moved to the Bronxdale Houses from a tenement in the South Bronx. These New York City housing projects were built in the 1940s and 1950s for working-class families as a step up from their old neighborhoods. The Bronxdale Houses consisted of twenty-eight buildings of seven stories each and were well maintained and safe. The grounds were landscaped and attractive, and the homes were clean. Sotomayor recalls that when they first moved in, she pedaled her tricycle around the spacious white-walled apartment and slammed into a wall, leaving a black mark. She was so scared that she had ruined the wall, she hid under the bed for a couple of hours.

The tenants at the Bronxdale Houses came from diverse backgrounds. Half were white (a mixture of Italian, Jewish, and Irish), about 30 percent were black, and 20 percent were Puerto Rican. The neighbors were friendly and looked after each other. It was so safe, residents would leave their doors propped open to catch a breeze (in the days before air conditioning units) and their bikes downstairs without locks.

Hard Times

When Sonia was eight, she was diagnosed with type 1 diabetes, a disorder caused by the body producing little or no insulin, a hormone that helps cells absorb glucose for energy. Blood glucose (or sugar) levels have to be monitored several times a day, and, depending on the glucose level, insulin must be injected. Celina tested Sonia's blood sugar and gave her daughter daily injections of insulin. As she grew older, Sonia began to monitor and inject herself, which she continues to do to this day to manage her condition.

Meanwhile, Juan Sotomayor, who spoke only Spanish, was in ill health from the heart disease that had kept him out of the army when he was a young man. When Sonia was nine, he died suddenly, most likely from a heart attack, at the age of forty-two. Celina was left a widow with two young children and as the sole support of her family. She started working six days a week and took a second job. The family moved to a smaller apartment in the Bronxdale Houses, and Sonia and Juan shared a room.

Celina used whatever money she could save to send the children to private Catholic school. The kids went to Blessed Sacrament, and Celina could spot them from their second-floor apartment when they walked home. She also thought it was worthwhile to purchase a set of *Encyclopedia Britannica* for the children to use at home. Homework was the kids' first priority. Only after it was finished could Sonia and Juan watch television, read, or listen to music.

Early Influences

Celina Sotomayor was the primary role model for her children. "I have often said that I am all I am because of her, and I am only half the woman she is," Sotomayor said on the day of her nomination to the Supreme Court. "I thank you for all that you have given me and continue to give me,"[12] she told her mother.

Juvenile Diabetes

Sonia Sotomayor was diagnosed with type 1 diabetes in 1962 when she was eight years old. According to writer Nancy Shute in *U.S. News and World Report*, "The number of children with type 1 diabetes continues to rise and doctors don't know why. . . . About 3 million Americans have type 1 diabetes now and 30,000 are diagnosed each year, about half of them children."[1]

Kids with diabetes "have to pay a little more attention to what they're eating and doing than kids without diabetes."[2] They have to check their blood sugar several times a day and give themselves insulin shots (or have their parents or the school nurse do it). They need to eat three meals a day of healthy, well-balanced food and exercise regularly. They may have to have a snack in the afternoon and should not skip meals. Otherwise, they can participate in sports, go to movies and restaurants, and do everything else kids do. The good news is that type 1 diabetes is manageable, and Sotomayor is a great example of that.

1. Nancy Shute, "With Type 1 Diabetes on the Rise, Parents Should Know the Warning Signs," *U.S. News and World Report*, May 28, 2009.

2. Kids Health, "Type 1 Diabetes: What Is It?" http://kidshealth .org/kid/health_problems/ gland/type1.html#.

In 1962 when she was eight years old Sonia was diagnosed with type 1 diabetes.

Sotomayor was fascinated with the Nancy Drew: Girl Detective books. Her first goal was to become a detective.

But as a young girl, Sotomayor was also influenced by what she read and by what she watched on television.

First written in 1930 and still published today, the Nancy Drew: Girl Detective series of books fascinated young Sonia, and her first career goal was to be a detective. Nancy "was the embodiment of independence, pluck, and intelligence,"[13] and Sonia loved settling down and reading such titles as *The Mystery of the Old Clock* and *The Clue of the Velvet Locket*.

After she was diagnosed with diabetes, she was told the life of a detective would be too physically demanding. Sonia discovered her next career choice by watching the television show *Perry Mason*. She noticed that defense attorney Mason was always able to prove his client's innocence by pointing out the guilt of another character. Sonia watched the show week after week and decided to become a lawyer. Eventually, she noticed that the judge had the most power in the courtroom, and she decided to be a judge.

"There were no lawyers or judges or even teachers in our family when we were growing up. . . . From television, I learned about lawyers and I dreamed about becoming a lawyer and a judge. . . . I've lived my dream," Sotomayor told a group of students at Stamford Middle School in the fall of 2004. "I wake up excited every morning about what I do," she said. "I have a voice in interpreting laws that affect people's lives. . . . The law and courts don't just put people in jail. We resolve the disputes, the fights that people have between them. We protect the legal right of individuals and organizations, poor and rich."[14]

Cultural Roots in the Bronx

As a child, Sotomayor spent a lot of time at her grandmother's apartment in the Bronx. She recalled childhood memories in her 2007 "Wall of Fame" speech. "My grandmother lived . . . on the top floor of a walk-up," she related, "and when I was little, my . . . legs would hurt before I reached the top and like most kids, I was too selfish to wonder how my grandmother did it every day, but she did."[15] Her apartment was close to the subway, and Sotomayor explained how the walls shook whenever a train went by. The New York City subway travels on elevated tracks in parts of the Bronx. Looking out the window of her grandmother's apartment, she and her cousins could see the faces of the people on the subway and would often wonder who they were, where they were going, and what kind of lives they lived. "I spent hours at that window looking at those people. We would make faces at them and then we could run away to the back of the apartment,"[16] she said.

Sotomayor also talked about going to the Spanish movie theatre down the block every Saturday afternoon for a double feature with her aunt and her cousins. "Titi [Auntie] Gloria had the most uncanny ability to walk in, in the last half of the first movie, sit through the first half of the second movie, and then make us leave," laughed Sotomayor. "I don't think that I have ever seen a Spanish movie from beginning to end. It used to drive me nuts."[17]

A Hard Worker

When Sonia Sotomayor was in high school (1968–1972), the nation was caught up in the turmoil of the civil rights movement and the Vietnam War. Like many young people around the country, she and other students were involved in the issues of the day. Sotomayor excelled on the debate team and in student government at Spellman High and was an obvious leader. She also worked hard to help her family and took many jobs on the weekends and during the summers.

In a 1994 interview with Channel 41, a Spanish-language station in New York, Sotomayor spoke directly to young people about education and jobs. "Go to school. Don't drop out," she said.

> You have to work hard. . . . There's nothing in life that's handed to anybody. I've been working since I was 14 years old. I've done just about every kind of work any kid out there will do. I've waited on tables, I've cleaned up slop, I've worked in bakeries, and dress shops and business offices, and consumer offices and manual and physical and mental labor. Sometimes I had two and three jobs. . . . And it didn't matter how hard I was working because I felt that I was getting something in return. . . . I got the ability to make my dreams come true. . . . You've got to give yourself the chance.

Sonia Sotomayor, "Interview with Channel 41, Part 2," October 1994, *New York Times* Video Library. http://video.nytimes.com/video/2009/06/10/us/politics/1194840839964/part-2-interview-with-channel-41.html.

Fun, Food, and Family

On Saturday nights, the extended Sotomayor family gathered at her grandmother's apartment. The adults played dominos, and the children played bingo, using chickpeas to mark the numbers, which her grandmother called out. For parties and special occasions, there was merengue, fast dance music that originated in the Dominican Republic, and "*mucho platos de arroz, gandoles y pernir*—[plenty of] rice, beans, and pork." Some of Sotomayor's favorite dishes included "*morcilla*,—pig intestines, *patitas de cerdo con garbanzo*—pigs' feet with beans, and *la lengua y orejas de cuchifrito*, pigs' tongue and ears."[18]

Sotomayor's mother, brother, and extended family played a vital role in her development and education while growing up. "They taught me to love being a Puerto Riqueña," she said, "and to love America and value its lesson that great things could be achieved if one works hard for it."[19] Sotomayor visited relatives in Puerto Rico regularly as a child and has continued to do so as an adult.

Time to Leave

The Sotomayor's neighborhood began to change slowly in the late 1960s. It was the "center of the universe" for the young Sotomayor, but "the Bronx was burning down," she said. "Drugs were so rampant [widespread] that on Saturday nights the police

On Saturday nights the extended Sotomayor family got together for fun and games at their grandmother's home. Sonia is pictured second from right.

locked down Southern Blvd. They made you stay inside."[20] First, heroin invaded the projects, then drug-dealing gangs. Waves of people moved to better neighborhoods farther north. According to Robin Shulman in the *New York Times*, "Landlords were setting fire to their own buildings because they could get more insurance money than rent" in other neighborhoods, and more strangers moved to the Bronxdale Houses.[21]

By the 1980s, Shulman notes, "the projects had become environments of concentrated poverty."[22] Today, violent gangs in the Bronxdale Houses make it much harder for kids to get out of the projects, but some still do.

Sonia was accepted into Cardinal Spellman High School in 1968, one of the top schools in the city, and by 1970, when she was sixteen, the family decided it was time to leave the Bronxdale Houses. They moved to a new, safer apartment in Co-op City, another neighborhood in the Bronx. Celina took the smaller bedroom and Juan and Sonia split the larger room. At this time, Celina went back to school to get her registered nurse's degree. The social security benefits the children had been receiving since their father's death would end when Juan graduated from high school, and Celina wanted to get a better job to make up for the loss of benefits.

Role Model

Sotomayor has a deep respect for her mother. In speeches and interviews she often talks about her mother's strength and determination. Sotomayor wrote in 1998, "She got home from school or work and literally immersed herself in her studies, working until midnight or beyond, only to get up again before all of us."[23] Celina became the emergency room supervisor at Prospect Hospital until it closed in 1985. Then she was a nurse at a methadone clinic in the South Bronx. She met and married Omar Lopez, and in the 1990s moved to a retirement community in Margate, Florida.

"If my mother's story teaches anything, it is that with education you can overcome enormous disadvantages,"[24] Sotomayor said in a commencement speech at Lehman College/City University of New York in 1999. Those words would also apply to Sotomayor herself. She graduated from Spellman High School

An Affirmative Action Baby

affirmative action: Special treatment for women and minorities in employment and college admissions to make up for past bigotry and prejudice.

Sotomayor received a scholarship to one of the top-rated universities in the country, despite having a somewhat lower SAT (Scholastic Aptitude Test) score than other students. She talked about being a "product of affirmative action" when she was a panelist in the early 1990s at the Practicing Law Institute. The topic was "Facing the 90s as a Woman Lawyer."

"I am the perfect affirmative action baby," Sotomayor explained.

> I am a Puerto Rican born and raised in the South Bronx and from what is traditionally described as a socio-economically poor background. My test scores were not comparable to that of my colleagues at Princeton or Yale—not so far off the mark that I wasn't able to succeed at those institutions, but if we had gone through the traditional numbers route . . . it would have been highly questionable whether I would have been accepted with my academic achievement in high school. . . . There are cultural biases built into testing and that was one of the motivations for the concept of affirmative action to try to balance out those effects.

Sonia Sotomayor, "Facing the 90s as a Woman Lawyer," panelist at Practicing Law Institute, early 1990s, *New York Times* Video Library. http://video.nytimes.com/video/2009/06/10/us/politics/1194840834851/practicing-law-institute-panelist.html.

in 1972 as the valedictorian of her class and got a full scholarship to attend college at Princeton University. Sotomayor left the comfort of her family and her urban neighborhood. She traveled about 60 miles (96.6km) to suburban New Jersey to attend the beautiful Ivy League campus of Princeton.

Chapter 2

Academic Activist: Rediscovering Her Roots

Princeton University was founded in 1746 as the College of New Jersey. The name was changed to Princeton in 1896. The campus has ivy-covered buildings and tree-lined streets. Shrubs, foliage, and walking paths surround the large dormitories, buildings, and towers. Apart from visits to Puerto Rico, Sotomayor knew only the urban landscape of the Bronx. When she set foot on the Princeton campus, she said it was like "a visitor landing in an alien country."[25]

A Different World

Most of the students at Princeton were financially well off and spoke about traveling to Europe on vacations or going to ski resorts. Many had parents or family members who had attended Princeton or other Ivy League schools. Princeton had only recently become a coed institution, so not only were comparatively few Latinos and other minorities on campus when Sotomayor arrived, but also far fewer women than men. It was unfamiliar territory to Sotomayor, and she has said that she felt quite overwhelmed, out of place, and intimidated by the situation.

According to CNN.com, during her first week on campus Sotomayor, a history major, was distressed by the sounds of

crickets at night. She thought the insects were hidden some-
where inside her dorm room, when they were actually outside
in the shrubbery. In the South Bronx, she was accustomed to
the honking of car horns, the hum of traffic, and sounds of
pedestrians talking, shouting, and laughing—typical noises in
a large vibrant city. At Princeton, insect sounds were magni-
fied in the quiet, still nights. "This was all new to me," said
Sotomayor in a speech to the Princeton Women's Network in
2002. "We didn't have trees brushing up against windows in
the South Bronx."[26]

Help with Academics

Despite an excellent record in high school, Spanish was Sotomayor's primary language at home until her father passed away
in 1963. As a freshman in college, she quickly became aware that
her written and oral skills were not as polished as those of some
of her classmates. She hardly spoke in class that first year.

According to writers Jodi Kantor and David Gonzalez of the
New York Times, "Sotomayor shut herself in her dorm room
and eventually resorted to grade-school grammar textbooks to
relearn her syntax." Some on campus believed that many female and minority students did not deserve to be at Princeton.
"They were subject to constant suspicion,"[27] write Kantor and

Sotomayor became involved in student activism at Princeton.

SONIA MARIA SOTOMAYOR

I am not a champion of lost causes, but of causes
not yet won.
— Norman Thomas

My Princeton experience has been the people I've met.
To them, for their lessons of life, I remain
eternally indebted and appreciative.
To them and to that extra-special person in my life

Thank You — For all that I am and am not.
The sum total of my life here, has been made-up
of little parts from all of you.

The Ivy League and the Big Three

Princeton University is one of eight universities in the northeast that make up the Ivy League. They include Brown in Providence, Rhode Island; Columbia in New York City; Cornell in Ithaca, New York; Dartmouth in Hanover, New Hampshire; Harvard in Cambridge, Massachusetts; University of Pennsylvania in Philadelphia, Pennsylvania; Princeton in Princeton, New Jersey; and Yale in New Haven, Connecticut. These schools are among the most prestigious and highest-rated academic institutions in the United States. Within the Ivy League, most consider the best three schools to be Harvard, Yale, and Princeton. These "Big Three" are the country's top-rated universities.

Princeton is one of eight universities that make up the Ivy League.

Gonzalez. Views like these made Sotomayor even more determined to better herself. She read books she had missed in high school, such as *Pride and Prejudice*, *Alice in Wonderland*, and *Huckleberry Finn*. She worked with several history professors to improve her vocabulary and develop her writing and critical thinking skills. Sotomayor spent many extra hours in the library and gradually gained confidence in her abilities.

Her freshman roommate was a Latina named Dolores Chavez from Albuquerque, New Mexico. They were from different backgrounds but became good friends. Chavez played the guitar and introduced Sotomayor to Mexican foods. Sotomayor brought Chavez home to the Bronx, fed her Puerto Rican food, and showed her around New York City.

Embracing Her Identity

By her sophomore year, Sotomayor was again confident in her academic abilities. This led to more openness and assertiveness in her personality. In a speech at Princeton in 1996, she declared, "My days at Princeton—were the single most transforming experience I have had. It was here that I became truly aware of my Latina identity—something I had taken for granted during my childhood when I was surrounded by my family and their friends."[28]

Sotomayor got involved in the student activist group, Acción Puertorriqueña (Puerto Rican Action), and became one of its co-chairs. She and other minority leaders on campus spoke with the president of the university, William G. Bowen, about the lack of Latino faculty members and the small numbers of minority students on campus. After no action was taken by the administration, Sotomayor wrote a follow-up letter, again without a response. Then she drafted a formal complaint and got the support of Frank Reed, the leader of Princeton's Chicano Caucus, another student group. Together, they officially filed a grievance with the federal government in April 1974, accusing Princeton of an "institutional pattern of discrimination" and "lack of commitment" in hiring "Puerto Rican and Chicano"[29] professors and recruiting Latino students.

In a letter to the *Daily Princetonian* on May 10, 1974, Sotomayor listed the Latino students' complaints:

> 1) There is not one Puerto Rican or Chicano administrator or faculty member in the university; 2) There are two million Puerto Ricans in the United States and two and a half million more on the island itself. Yet there were only 66 Puerto Rican applicants this year, and only 31 Puerto Rican students on campus. While there are 12 million Chicanos in the United States, there were only 111 Chicano applicants and 27 students on campus this year; 3) Not one permanent course in this university now deals in any notable detail with the Puerto Rican or Chicano cultures.[30]

Working Within the System

Although Princeton had an affirmative action plan in 1974, the student groups claimed the plan had no scheduled timelines or goals for hiring Hispanics. The administration's affirmative actions officer admitted, "We can make better efforts in the future."[31] Before an official ruling was made by the government on the students' complaint, Princeton began to hire more minority staff members (including the first Hispanic dean of students) and accepted increased numbers of Latino students.

Writers Evan Thomas, Stuart Taylor Jr., and Brian No declared in a *Newsweek* article that Princeton "taught . . . [Sotomayor] how to play a particular sort of power game, to get ahead the Princeton way—not by assertion or bullying, but by reason and carefully prepared persuasion. . . . Change is to be achieved by working within the system, not by tearing things down."[32] When others argued to demonstrate, take over buildings, or hand out leaflets, Sotomayor kept talking with administrators in addition to going through the legal system.

Bowen told *Newsweek*, "What I remember most was just how mature she was. We didn't see her as wanting to do anything except to improve the university," he said. "She was not one of those students who pushed herself on you." Bowen referred to Sotomayor as a "true all-rounder,"[33] a student who combined leadership and scholarship.

Other Activities at Princeton

Sotomayor supported gay rights and spoke out against police abuse and violence in public housing projects. She served on the Governance Board of the Third World Center, helped to form a Latino Students Organization, and volunteered at the Trenton Psychiatric Hospital as an interpreter.

In her junior year, Sotomayor was one of a group who persuaded history professor Peter Winn to develop a class on Puerto Rican history and politics. She worked many jobs on campus, including at the school cafeteria and the Third World Center. She also took a work-study job in the admissions office that allowed her to travel to area high schools to recruit outstanding Latino students for Princeton.

Sotomayor's undergraduate thesis at Princeton was on the first elected governor of Puerto Rico, Luis Muñoz Marín, and his place in Puerto Rican political history.

Her undergraduate thesis focused on Luis Muñoz Marín, the first governor of Puerto Rico elected by popular vote. It was titled, "The Impact of the Life of Luis Muñoz Marín on the Political and Economic History of Puerto Rico, 1930–1975." Sotomayor was elected to Phi Beta Kappa (the academic honor society) in her senior year and won the university's prestigious Pyne Prize, the top award for an undergraduate at Princeton. She graduated in 1976 with a degree in history, summa cum laude (with highest praise—maintaining a grade point average of 3.8 or better).

Sotomayor had had an ongoing relationship with Kevin Noonan since high school and throughout her years at Princeton. She married him in August 1976 at St. Patrick's Cathedral in New York City. She then headed off to Yale Law School in New Haven, Connecticut, another Ivy League school, after winning a scholarship.

Polished and Confident at Yale

For Sotomayor, arriving at Yale was very different from her early experiences at Princeton. She became comfortable very quickly, despite the small number of Hispanics in the law school class of 160 students. She no longer felt intimidated but was secure in her ability to compete with her classmates. According to writers Peter Nicholas and James Oliphant in the *Los Angeles Times*, "Sotomayor immersed herself in the law—and fused it to her Latina identity. . . . And as she had done at Princeton, she found ways to engage in advocacy."[34]

One of the first things Sotomayor did after arriving in New Haven was to call José Cabranes, the university's general counsel, who also happened to be Puerto Rican. She was referred to him by one of her Princeton professors. Cabranes hired her as an intern and research assistant for a book he was working on about the history of Puerto Rico. "Jose Cabranes . . . was her most influential early mentor,"[35] writes *Washington Post* staffer Amy Goldstein. He went on to become Sotomayor's colleague as a Second Circuit Court of Appeals judge.

At Yale, Sotomayor joined the Latino, Asian, and Native American Students Association. She became cochair of the group and met with the dean of the law school to promote the recruitment of more minority students and the hiring of more minority faculty. She was an editor on the *Yale Law Journal*, managing editor of the *Yale Studies in World Public Order*, and had a law review note (short article) published that analyzed the effects of possible Puerto Rican statehood on mineral rights to the island's surrounding seabed.

The First Lady's Similar Experience

Sonia Sotomayor was at Princeton from 1972 to 1976. First Lady of the United States Michelle Obama was at Princeton from 1981 to 1985, yet their experiences were very similar. Cheryl Nix Hines, a classmate of Obama's, told the website Politico that "Like Judge Sotomayor, Michelle Obama had to find her comfort zone in a community of extraordinarily intelligent and privileged individuals at Princeton, most of whom had little knowledge of the circumstances from which she had risen."

Obama wrote in her thesis introduction that her "experiences at Princeton have made me far more aware of my 'blackness' than ever before. . . . I sometimes feel like a visitor on campus; as if I really don't belong." She continued, "Regardless of the circumstances under which I interact with whites at Princeton, it often seems as if, to them, I will always be black first and a student second."

Both Sotomayor's and Obama's experiences at Princeton pushed them into exploring their own roots and the politics that went with them. Their respective Latino and African American heritages gave each of them a renewed sense of racial identity and helped anchor and shape their adulthood.

Quoted in Ben Smith, "Princeton Key to Knowing Sotomayor," Politico, May 29, 2009. http://dyn.politico.com/printstory.cfm?uuid=8A0B1C0B-18FE-70B2-A87EA 1059B2EA0C6.

An Offensive Question

In the fall of her last year of law school, Sotomayor attended a recruiting dinner. A number of private firms came on campus to interview third-year students about possible employment after graduation. The dinner was a social event preceding the formal interviews the following day. An attorney from the private Washington firm of Shaw, Pittman, Potts & Trowbridge asked Sotomayor if she would have been admitted to Yale if she were not Puerto Rican. She felt that the lawyer was suggesting she was at Yale only because of her ethnicity and not her excellent record at Princeton, and found the question insulting and offensive.

During her formal interview the next day, Sotomayor explained to the firm's representative that she believed the question was discriminatory. She refused to travel to Washington for a second interview, and she made a formal complaint against the firm to the assistant dean of the law school. Sotomayor was supported

Manhattan district attorney Robert Morgenthau hired Sotomayor as an assistant district attorney fresh out of Yale Law School in 1980.

by student groups at Yale that wanted the firm prohibited from campus recruitment. A faculty-student tribunal ruled in her favor. The firm apologized for the lawyer's behavior, and the incident was reported in the *Washington Post*.

She'll Take Manhattan

Sotomayor received her JD (juris doctor) degree from Yale Law School in 1979 and was admitted to the New York State bar in 1980. Cabranes helped her get her first job. He knew Manhattan district attorney Robert Morgenthau from their days together on the Puerto Rican Legal Defense and Education Fund (now called LatinoJustice PRLDEF). Cabranes recommended Sotomayor to Morgenthau because he thought she would enjoy trial work as an assistant district attorney in Morgenthau's office. Morgenthau was impressed and hired the young Latina. While most Princeton Law School graduates went into private practice or other high-paying jobs, Sotomayor returned to the Big Apple to practice law in the public sector at a time when New York's crime rates and drug problems were soaring to a crisis level.

Chapter 3

Criminal Law, Civil Law, and Public Service: Gaining Experience

A crime wave was rolling through New York City at the time Sonia Sotomayor started work as an assistant district attorney in Manhattan. The city was on the verge of bankruptcy, fires were deliberately being set in the Bronx and Brooklyn, and drug dealers sold their wares openly in tenement buildings in lower Manhattan. According to *New York Times* writers Benjamin Weiser and William K. Rashbaum, "Dealers would set up shop on the top floors of tenements on the Lower East Side and lines of addicts would snake down the steps and outside onto the street."[36]

The annual homicide rate had spiraled to nearly two thousand victims, more than three times the number it is today. The district attorneys (DAs) and the police department spent their time fighting crime, dealing with victims and their families, and trying to convince frightened witnesses to come forward. Over three hundred assistant DAs were in the Manhattan office in the early 1980s, and they usually handled dozens of cases at a time.

A Busy Prosecutor

Sotomayor earned about seventeen thousand dollars when she first started working for Morgenthau. He was a well-known figure who had been U.S. attorney for the Southern District of New York under three presidents (Kennedy, Johnson, and Nixon) before becoming Manhattan's DA in 1975. Despite the fact that law school graduates could earn double the salary in private practice, their applications to the DA's office far outnumbered its available job openings. The main attraction, aside from

As a Manhattan assistant district attorney, Sotomayor successfully prosecuted Richard Maddicks, the Tarzan Burglar.

gaining valuable experience for future law jobs, was trying cases before juries, putting criminals behind bars, and working for a legendary figure like Morgenthau. Morgenthau retired in 2009 at age ninety after thirty-five years as the head of what the *New York Times* called the "country's premier prosecutorial office."[37]

At first, Sotomayor handled misdemeanors such as shoplifting, prostitution, and minor assault cases. "In large measure, in those cases you were dealing with socioeconomic crimes, crimes that could be the product of the environment and of poverty,"[38] explained the then twenty-nine-year-old assistant DA in a *New York Times Magazine* article in 1983. Six months later, Sotomayor was working violent felonies in Trial Bureau 50.

Bureau head Warren Murray once said, "If you can handle a felony case load in New York County, you can run a small country."[39] Sotomayor's most significant case as a prosecutor was one of the most publicized and her first murder case. She assisted a more experienced assistant DA named Hugh Mo.

The Tarzan Burglar

Between 1981 and 1982, a criminal in central Harlem used ropes and cables attached to rooftops to break into top-floor apartments. The man came crashing through windows to rob and murder "with guns blazing"[40] at whoever got in his way; hence, the nickname Tarzan, the fictional character who swung on vines through the jungle. By the time the police arrested the man, who was named Richard Maddicks, he had murdered three people, injured six more, and was involved in more than twenty-five burglaries. Mo and Sotomayor were assigned the Tarzan case, and Sotomayor visited the scenes of the crimes, interviewed dozens of witnesses, and put together a set of facts and events that linked the accused to the murders and burglaries.

She examined and cross-examined twenty of the forty witnesses (Mo questioned the others) before a judge and jury. Witnesses included pathologists (who study diseases) and ballistics experts (who study the motion of bullets) as well as the family members of victims and those who heard or saw anything relating to the crimes and the defendant.

Bulletproof Vests and Motorcycle Chases

Sotomayor described her experiences working for Pavia & Harcourt in a speech at an IACC (International Anti-Counterfeiting Coalition) luncheon in October 1997:

> My practice at Pavia had been quite diverse and stimulating. . . . My investigative experience with the Manhattan D.A.'s office came in handy when I found myself doing anti-counterfeiting work on behalf of Fendi and other trademark owners. . . . I particularly enjoyed the many lovely afternoons in Chinatown spent wearing a bulletproof vest . . . seizing counterfeit goods from the nooks and crannies many of us never imagined existed within the maze of buildings that is Chinatown.[1]

Sotomayor also spoke of "the pleasant afternoon . . . outside Shea Stadium chasing counterfeiters around the parking lot on motorcycles. I have never gotten back on a motorcycle after that day when I belatedly realized that cars were much bigger than motorcycles and that I had lost reason in the heat of pursuit by ever getting on the motorcycle as a passenger at all to chase the vans that stored the counterfeit goods. . . . "

Not all of Sotomayor's practice involved police seizures and motorcycle chases. She dealt with basic legal matters that make up most of a lawyer's work. In a 1986 *Good Morning America* television interview, Sotomayor declared that "the vast majority of lawyering is drudgery work . . . it's sitting in a library, it's banging out a brief, it's talking to clients for endless hours."[2]

1. Sonia Sotomayor, speech to IACC, October 16, 1997, William J. Clinton National Presidential Library collection, "Sotomayor—Supplement to Senate," NLWFC-Sotomayor-Box0003-Folder00008, FOIA Number 2009-1007-F, OA/ID Number 12690.

2. Sonia Sotomayor, interview on *Good Morning America*, *New York Times* Video Library, 1986. http://video.nytimes.com/video/2009/06/10/us/politics/1194840839411/interview-on-good-morning-america.html.

Sotomayor managed to get Maddicks's girlfriend to testify against him in exchange for a reduced sentence for her involvement in another case. Sotomayor also linked the murder weapon to Maddicks through a neighbor's testimony in court. When she questioned a girlfriend of one of the murder victims, every member of the jury was in tears. Sotomayor used a chart that linked the defendant to the crimes as a visual aid to the jurors. Maddicks was convicted and is serving 62 years to life in prison.

Other Notable Cases

Sotomayor listed the Tarzan Burglar case as among the ten most significant court cases of her career as an attorney. Two others also came from her days in the district attorney's office. One was the first child pornography conviction after a Supreme Court decision in *People v. Ferber*, which upheld a New York State law that prohibited the selling of sexually explicit films with children in them. Two men went to prison for selling child porn out of a bookstore in Manhattan. Another case involved a shooting in a housing project, and the successful prosecution and conviction of one of the defendants in the case.

Morgenthau remarked that when Sotomayor worked for him, "She was always a step ahead of the rest of us. She was a quick study, a very hard worker, a very good lawyer, and she just did extremely well."[41] In 1983 Sotomayor declared in the *New York Times Magazine*, "It pains me when I meet particularly bright defendants . . . people who, if they had had the right guidance, the right education, the right breaks, could have been contributing members of our society. When they get convicted," she said, "there's a satisfaction, because they're doing things that are dangerous. But there are also nights when I sit back and say, 'My God, what a waste!'"[42]

Private Practice: Pavia & Harcourt

After nearly five years on the front lines of the criminal justice system, Sotomayor decided to move on to private practice in civil law. Not only could she earn more money but would ex-

Ninety-year-old Robert Morgenthau (right) testifies before the U.S. Senate Judiciary Committee in support of Sotomayor. He said that "she was always a step ahead of the rest of us."

pand her knowledge and practice of the law in a different area. She told the *New York Times* in a 1985 interview, "After a while, you forget there are decent, law-abiding people in life. In one of the last cases I had, for gun possession, I thought I recognized the defendant's name. So I looked at his sheet and, sure enough, he was one of the first defendants I had had."[43] With the help and support of Morgenthau, Sotomayor was hired at the law firm of Pavia & Harcourt in New York City in 1984.

According to its website, Pavia & Harcourt was established in 1940 as a business law firm concentrating in commercial and corporate law, banking, media and entertainment, real estate, litigation and arbitration, and intellectual property, among other things. The firm's attorneys are fluent in Spanish, French, Portuguese, and Italian, and represent foreign companies and individuals who do business in the United States, as well as American clients who do business abroad.

The intellectual property section, of which Sotomayor was a part, developed and managed anticounterfeiting programs and tried cases that involved trademarks, copyrighted works, and designs. Working closely with the police and law enforcement, civil actions were brought against counterfeiters and infringers of trademarks and copyrights, and goods were seized. She traveled in the United States and abroad working for American and European clients. A 1984 federal law allowed for the civil seizure of counterfeit goods off the streets. Sotomayor was one of several attorneys who helped to write anticounterfeiting legislation that eventually became part of the New York State penal code (Sec. 165.70–74). Sotomayor also worked in automobile franchising and grain commodity trading at Pavia, but the intellectual property part was most enjoyable for her.

One of her major clients was Fendi, the Italian designer of luxury handbags. Sotomayor represented Fendi in its fight against vendors who sold phony handbags for low prices on the streets of New York City with fake double-F Fendi logos. The effort to crack down on fake goods culminated in an event called the "Fendi Crush" in which Carla Fendi oversaw the crushing of thousands of seized counterfeit bags and accessories in garbage trucks. In 1987 Sotomayor represented Fendi in suing the Burlington Coat Factory, and the case was settled out of court. Her fluency in Spanish was very helpful in learning basic Italian, which allowed her to communicate not only with Fendi but also with the Italian car dealer and manufacturer Ferrari. In 1990 Sotomayor represented Ferrari North America in a dispute with a California car dealership and won the case.

Ardent Civil Advocate

After she started work in the DA's office, Cabranes encouraged her to stay active and join the board of the Puerto Rican Legal Defense and Education Fund in New York (now known as LatinoJustice PRLDEF). Sotomayor was on the board of directors from 1980 until 1992 and met twice a month with PRLDEF lawyers to discuss legal tactics and priorities. Cesar Perales, the

Moving On in Her Personal Life

When Sotomayor started the job in New York City in 1979 after law school, her husband, Kevin Noonan, had a residence in Princeton and attended graduate school there. On many occasions, Sotomayor had to work late or be in court early and could not travel the two hours back to or from Princeton. An attorney friend, Nancy Gray, let her stay at her apartment in New York when she needed to.

Noonan eventually followed his academic adviser to Chicago, while his wife's career in New York was rising. They were moving in different directions and mutually agreed to a divorce in 1983. Years later, Sotomayor explained the situation when she was on a judicial panel about women lawyers in the 1990s. "I cannot attribute that divorce to work," she said, "but certainly the fact that I was leaving my home at 7 and getting back at 10 o'clock was not of assistance in recognizing the problems developing in my marriage."[1]

Sotomayor was later in a long relationship with Peter White, a construction and architectural consultant, and they were engaged to be married. The relationship ended in the late 1990s. White told Amy Goldstein of the *Washington Post*, "She is extremely dedicated to her work, which takes up 90 percent of the time. There wasn't room for two careers in one household."[2]

1. Quoted in Michael Powell, Serge F. Kovaleski, and Russ Buettner, "To Get to Sotomayor's Core, Start in New York," *New York Times*, July 10, 2009. www.nytimes .com/2009/07/10/nyregion/10sonia.html?pagewanted=print.

2. Quoted in Amy Goldstein, "A Steady Rise, Punctuated by Doubts," *Washington Post*, July 12, 2009. www.washingtonpost.com/wp-dyn/content/article/2009/07/11/ AR2009071102788_pf.html.

PRLDEF's cofounder and executive director in the 1980s, describes Sotomayor and the other lawyers in a *Washington Post* article as "people who very much believed in social justice and the use of the law to achieve social justice."[44]

Cofounder and director of PRLDEF in the 1980s, Cesar Perales stated that Sotomayor very much believed in social justice and worked against the death penalty while part of the organization's legal team.

Sotomayor played an active role in legal issues involving voting rights and police brutality. She was part of a PRLDEF committee that opposed the death penalty in New York and supported the committee's statement that capital punishment was related to racism in society.

One lawsuit charged discrimination against minority candidates in a New York City police department promotional exam. Whites scored higher on the test than Hispanics and African Americans. The PRLDEF, on behalf of the Hispanic Society of NY Police, charged the exams were unfair and did not actually measure performance. The result was a settlement with the city and more promotions for minority officers. The white officers who scored high on the exam sued, and the case *Marino v. Ortiz* went all the way to the U.S. Supreme Court in 1988. It failed with a tie vote of 4-4.

Focus on the Poor and Low-Income Families

By the late 1980s Sotomayor was known in New York as an excellent, caring, and hard-working attorney. She believed that because she had so many opportunities in her life, she wanted to give back to those who did not have the same advantages. She also wanted to become a judge someday. As a panelist commenting on the topic "Facing the 90s as a Woman Lawyer," Sotomayor stated that "it is important as a practicing lawyer who aspires to be a judge, to insure that they get out there and get themselves known. . . . It means working on committees and doing substantive work so people can have an opportunity to judge your skills."[45]

Sotomayor had many good friends in high places, including Morgenthau and partners and clients of Pavia & Harcourt. In 1987 she was appointed by New York governor Mario Cuomo to the State Mortgage Agency Board, where she served until 1992. The agency helped to provide mortgage insurance to developers of large residential properties in low-income areas that had been devastated by fire and abandoned buildings. The city committed billions of dollars to rebuild these neighborhoods and required some portion of the new projects to offer affordable housing to low- and moderate-income families.

During her years on the board, Sotomayor was more concerned about poor and low-income families and the effect of what is called gentrification. Gentrification occurs when middle- or upper-class people buy housing in poorer neighborhoods and replace the low-income residents. The property is then restored and improved, resulting in increased property values and neighborhood upgrade. *New York Times* writers Charlie Savage and Michael Powell examined minutes of board meetings during the time Sotomayor was active. They note that "[Sotomayor] felt that economic development . . . [was] . . . displacing cultural groups who formed the original neighborhood," and "the project[s] [were] not adequately addressing the needs of low-income people."[46]

In 1990 Sotomayor objected to the rehabilitation of six buildings in the Bronx because they were aimed at residents making twenty-one thousand to twenty-nine thousand dollars per year. She was concerned because nearly 90 percent of residents of the surrounding communities earned less money than that. Angelo Aponte, another board member and former

Solo Law Practice: Sotomayer & Associates

From 1983 to 1986 Sonia Sotomayor ran a law practice out of her apartment in Brooklyn. On the questionnaire for judicial nominees that she submitted to the U.S. Senate Committee on the Judiciary, Sotomayor describes her practice: "This work was more in the nature of a consultant to family and friends in their real estate, business, and estate planning decisions. If their circumstances required formal legal representation I referred the matter to my firm, Pavia Harcourt, or to others with appropriate expertise."

Sonia Sotomayor, "Sonia Sotomayor Senate Questionnaire," Biographical Information-Response to Question 17a2, William J. Clinton National Presidential Library collection, "Sotomayor—Supplement to Senate," NLWFC-Sotomayor-Box0003-Folder00008, FOIA Number 2009-1007-F, OA/ID Number 1269.

state housing commissioner told the *Times* that Sotomayor "was the conscience of the board. She kept reminding the board and developers that . . . you have to keep in mind where you are building and whether people can afford to live there and not be shoved out of where they've been living for many years."[47] More than 309,000 apartments were either built or renovated in what Savage and Powell write was "one of the greatest urban rebuilding feats in the nation's history."[48]

Additional Public Service

In 1988 Sotomayor was made full partner at Pavia & Harcourt. That same year she was also one of the founding members appointed to New York City's new Campaign Finance Board by Mayor Ed Koch, which enforced election spending laws. According to Savage, "The board members, including Ms. Sotomayor, became pioneers in developing a voluntary program in which local candidates receive public matching money in exchange for accepting disclosure requirements and limits on contributions and spending."[49] Sotomayor also served on the board of the Maternity Center Association (now known as Childbirth Connection) in 1985–1986. This Manhattan group focused on improving the quality of maternity care.

The years of voluntary public service, along with her nearly eight years at Pavia & Harcourt in civil litigation and five years in the DA's office in criminal litigation, resulted in making Sotomayor an exceptionally well-rounded attorney in all aspects of the law. This was recognized by David Botwinik, a partner and mentor at her firm, who encouraged his colleague to apply for a federal judgeship. Sotomayor was hesitant, but after months of persistent encouragement by Botwinik and others, she filled out an application.

According to Amy Goldstein at the *Washington Post*, it was Botwinik who called "a childhood friend running a committee that New York's longtime Democratic Senator, Daniel Patrick Moynihan, had set up to screen possible candidates for federal

It was New York senator Daniel Patrick Moynihan, who, impressed with Sotomayor's knowledge, record, and character, initially recommended her for a federal judgeship.

judgeships."[50] Moynihan was impressed with Sotomayor's knowledge, record, and character. He was particularly pleased at the opportunity to appoint an outstanding young Latina attorney to the bench. At the age of thirty-seven, Sotomayor would soon experience her first Senate confirmation hearing.

Federal Judgeship: The Savior of Baseball

The two U.S. senators from New York, Democrat Daniel Patrick Moynihan and Republican Alfonse D'Amato, had a special arrangement with each other about federal judgeships. During a Republican administration, such as the one of President George H.W. Bush in 1991, Moynihan would get to choose one district judge for every three that D'Amato selected. With Moynihan's pick of Sonia Sotomayor, the Democrat could finally fulfill a promise he made to choose a Hispanic judge from the Empire State. Senator D'Amato supported Sotomayor and submitted her name to President Bush, who officially announced her nomination on November 29, 1991.

The Judiciary Committee hearings in the Senate went well, and Sotomayor got unanimous approval for a floor vote. However, her confirmation was held up for nine months by a Republican senator who used an anonymous hold to block her approval and that of three other nominees. (The block was in retaliation for a hold by Democrats). D'Amato objected to the hold, and it was eventually dropped. Sotomayor was finally confirmed by the full Senate on August 11, 1992. She became the youngest judge in the Southern District at age thirty-eight, the first Hispanic judge in the state of New York, and the first Puerto Rican to serve in the federal court system. To avoid any

Sotomayor was unanimously confirmed by the U.S. Senate on August 11, 1992. She became the first Hispanic judge in the state of New York and the first Puerto Rican to serve on the federal court.

conflict of interest, Sotomayor ended her active participation in the Puerto Rican Legal Defense and Education Fund, the New York City Campaign Finance Board, and the New York State Mortgage Agency when she became a judge.

All About the Federal Courts

The judicial branch of the government was established by the U.S. Constitution in Article III, which states, "The judicial power of the United States shall be vested in one supreme Court, and in such inferior Courts as the Congress may from time to time ordain and establish. The Judges, both of the supreme and inferior Courts, shall hold their Offices during good Behaviour, and shall, at stated Times, receive for their Services, a Compensation, which shall not be diminished during their Continuance in Office." The rulings of the federal courts protect the Constitutional rights of all Americans. According to the government pamphlet *Understanding the Federal Courts*, they "interpret and apply the law to resolve disputes,"[51] while Congress makes the laws and the President and the executive branch enforce them. Federal judges are appointed for life, and proceedings are open to the public.

The Supreme Court is the highest court in the land. Its justices hear a limited number of cases each term that involve important questions of federal or constitutional law. Second highest are the courts of appeals, with twelve regional circuits throughout the country. The district trial courts are at the lowest federal level, with ninety-four judicial districts. Supreme Court justices and judges at the district courts and courts of appeals are appointed by the president with the consent of the U.S. Senate.

Sotomayor became a federal judge for the Southern District of New York, which includes Manhattan and the Bronx in New York County, as well as Westchester, Putnam, Rockland, Orange, Dutchess, and Sullivan counties. She presided over trials of both civil and criminal matters in every category. For the most part, Sotomayor's term on the district court was low-key and noncontroversial. But several very high profile cases received much publicity in the media. The most publicized was

The Nomination Process

Sonia Sotomayor submitted the following details of her district judgeship nomination to the Senate Judiciary Committee in 1992. She wrote,

> At the suggestion of various friends, I submitted an application to and was interviewed by the Committee on the Judiciary which advises Senator Daniel Patrick Moynihan on his judicial recommendations. I subsequently met with Senator Moyhihan who then recommended me to Senator Alfonse D'Amato. Senator D'Amato forwarded my name to the Department of Justice. I was first contacted and interviewed by the Committee of the Judiciary of the Bar of the City of New York which approved my qualifications for the appointment. Thereafter, on two occasions, I was contacted by and met with various officials at the Department of Justice. I was then sent requisite forms which I completed. I was then interviewed by an agent of the Federal Bureau of Investigation and by a representative of the Standing Committee on the Federal Judiciary of the American Bar Association before my nomination by the President.

> Sotomayor next answered questions before the Senate Judiciary Committee, which had to approve her nomination before a full vote for confirmation was taken on the Senate floor.

Quoted in Garance Franke-Ruta, "Sotomayor's District Court Bid Aided by D'Amato and Moynihan," *Washington Post*, May 27, 2009.

the case of *Silverman v. Major League Baseball Player Relations Committee* in 1995 in which Sotomayor gained the title of the "savior of baseball."

Take Me Out to the Ball Game

Baseball players first obtained the right to free agency and salary arbitration in the 1970s. The free agency system allows players who have played six seasons or more in the major leagues to declare their free agency and then negotiate with other clubs in order to get the best salary, move to a different location, or go to a winning team—whatever is important to that player.

Those who have played for more than three major league seasons but less than six years are eligible for salary arbitration if they cannot reach an agreement with their clubs. If the dispute goes to salary arbitration, both the player and owner submit a salary figure to the arbitrator. Of the two figures, the arbitrator decides which one the ballplayer deserves on the basis of specific performance criteria. Both sides must accept the salary figure selected by the arbitrator.

From the 1970s into the 1990s, contract negotiations and labor relations between the owners and the players were hostile. The players believed the owners wanted to cut back free agency and other rights the players had obtained. A basic agreement between the owners and players ran from January 1990 through December 1993. Negotiations for a new agreement began in March 1994, and the season started in April 1994 under the terms of the previous expired agreement.

On Strike

Former major league pitcher David Cone, who spent eighteen years in baseball, described that 1994 season at the Sotomayor confirmation hearings on July 16, 2009. "The owners said that they wanted the salary cap [a limit on the amount of money a team could spend on the salaries of players] and refused to promise that they would abide by the rules of the just-expired contract after the season ended," explained Cone. "Believing we had no choice, the players went on strike in August of 1994."[52]

The owners responded to the players' strike by canceling the rest of the season, including playoffs and the World Series. Negotiations continued the rest of the year, but the sides could not reach agreement. "In December of 1994," stated Cone, "the owners . . . implemented a salary cap and imposed new rules and conditions on employment which would have made free agency virtually meaningless." He continued, "And they announced they would start the 1995 season with so-called replacement players instead of major leaguers."[53] The players' representatives believed the owners were not negotiating in good faith under federal law and went to the National Labor Relations Board (NLRB), which has the power "to prevent any person from engaging in any unfair labor practice."[54] The NLRB, on behalf of the baseball players, sought a temporary injunction, a court order prohibiting the action of the owners before legal questions are decided in federal court, and the judge assigned to the case was Sotomayor.

In Sotomayor's 2009 Senate confirmation hearings, former Major League Baseball player David Cone testified that during the 1994–1995 baseball strike Sotomayor's rulings in the case effectively saved Major League Baseball.

Play Ball!

Sotomayor found "just and proper cause to issue an injunction." She declared in her written decision,

> This strike is about more than just whether the Players and Owners will resolve their differences. It is also about how the principles embodied by federal labor law operate. In a very real and immediate way, this strike has placed the entire concept of collective bargaining on trial. It is critical, therefore, that the Board ensure that the spirit and letter of federal labor law be scrupulously followed.
>
> If the Board is unable to enforce the NLRA [National Labor Relations Act], public confidence in the collective bargaining process will be permanently and severely undermined. Issuing the injunction before Opening Day is important to ensure that the symbolic value of that day is not tainted by an unfair labor practice and the NLRB's inability to take effective steps against its perpetuation. . . . I find that the harm to the public, the players, and the NLRB compels the issuance of a[n] . . . injunction in this case.[55]

The Court of Appeals unanimously upheld her decision.

Sotomayor's ruling saved the 1995 baseball season and made the parties continue negotiations. The players voted to return to work, and the owners went back to the bargaining table after Sotomayor issued the temporary injunction that denied their proposed one-sided changes. The start of the 1995 baseball season was delayed from April 2 to April 25, and the season was shortened from 162 games to 144 games. The strike had lasted 232 days.

An agreement was finally reached in November 1996. Cone noted that "baseball is currently enjoying a run of more than 14 years without interruption, a record that would have been inconceivable in the 1990s. I believe all of us who have loved the game, players, owners and fans, are in her debt."[56] The Silverman v. Major League Baseball case brought Sotomayor fame, but she also presided over other interesting and notable cases during her term as a district judge.

The Public's Right to Know

In the 1995 case *Dow-Jones v. U.S. Department of Justice*, Sotomayor ruled in favor of Dow-Jones and against the Department of Justice. The decision allowed the *Wall Street Journal* (owned by Dow-Jones) to publish a photocopy of a suicide note written by White House deputy counsel Vince Foster, who served in President Bill Clinton's administration. He had been depressed and shot himself in 1993. The Department of Justice (DOJ) argued that "the Foster family's privacy interests outweigh[ed] any . . . public interest that would be served by disclosure of the Note" and that the note should be exempt from disclosure. Sotomayor disagreed. She wrote,

> The public has a substantial interest in viewing the Note. The matters discussed in the Note touched on several events of public interest. . . . According to statements made at the Press Conference, the Note was torn up by someone, and some of the pieces are missing. The missing pieces, the "look" of the handwriting, and the significance to be drawn therefrom, are . . . matters of public concern. . . . I do not doubt that making photocopies of the Note available on a wider scale may spark a new round of media attention toward the Foster family, and I sympathize with them for the pain they will bear as a result of any renewed scrutiny. I am not convinced, however, that any such renewed interest will be so substantial as to outweigh the important public interest in viewing the Note.

Sonia Sotomayor, *Dow-Jones & Company, Inc. v. United States Department of Justice*, U.S. District Court, Southern District New York, 880 F. Supp. 145, Jan. 5 1995.

Menorah in the Park

In *Flamer v. City of White Plains, New York*, 1993, Sotomayor dealt with issues of freedom of expression and freedom of religion. Rabbi Reuven Flamer tried to get permission from White

Plains to display a menorah during the eight-night Hanukkah holiday in one of the public parks. He was denied permission in 1991 and 1992 because of a council resolution that prohibited "fixed outdoor display[s] of religious or political symbols." Flamer challenged the city council resolution in 1993 and claimed it was unconstitutional under the First and Fourteenth Amendments dealing with free speech and equal protection under the law. The city argued that "permitting such a display now would violate the Establishment Clause [separation of church and state] because it would convey the impression that the City endorsed particular religions or religion generally."[57]

In the **Flamer v. City of White Plains, New York** *ruling, Sotomayor determined the City of White Plains violated Rabbi Flamer's First Amendment rights when it refused to let him display a menorah on public land.*

Sotomayor ruled that White Plains had violated Flamer's First Amendment rights. In the decision she noted that

> over the years, a wide array of expressive activity by private groups and individuals has occurred in both Tibbets and Main [the city's public parks]. A prime area for political expression, Main has been used by numerous political and social activist organizations for demonstrations, rallies and vigils, around issues as diverse as Middle East peace, the United States' invasion of Panama, abortion rights and nuclear disarmament. . . .

> For the reasonable observer, the private religious fixed display should be no different from other fixed displays erected by private speakers. This observer should understand that the public forum is the public's expressive playground, and that private speakers with a religious message, like any other member of the public, will resort to this forum to convey their particular messages.[58]

Sotomayor declared the council resolution unconstitutional and wrote that a reasonable observer would not conclude that the government endorsed a religion or point of view just because fixed displays were allowed in the public parks. Flamer was granted a permit to display the menorah during Hanukkah.

Baubles, Bangles, and Beads

Another freedom of religion case was *Campos v. Coughlin* in 1994. A New York State law prohibited prison inmates "from wearing religious medals, crucifixes, or crosses, attached to beads, leather, string or rope,"[59] because the beads, leather, or string could display gang-related colors or pose a security risk. However, the prisoners were allowed to wear traditional crosses, medals, and crucifixes on chains under their clothing.

Those prisoners who practiced Santeria (a Caribbean sect that combines parts of Roman Catholicism with African beliefs) were required by their religion to wear multicolored beads but

In Campos v. Coughlin, Sotomayor ruled that Santeria practitioners in prison could wear religious beads. To prevent them from doing so was a violation of the First and Fourteenth Amendments.

were prohibited by prison officials from doing so. Two inmates, Tony Campos and Alex Lance, filed a lawsuit claiming the policy denied them their religious freedom under the First and Fourteenth Amendments. "Only in the case of Santeria beads," wrote Sotomayor, "does the failure to wear them, according to plaintiffs' beliefs, result in negative and possibly irreversible life consequences for the practitioner."[60] She ruled that the prison's policy violated the men's constitutional rights and ordered New York State to allow inmates to wear the beads under their clothing.

Hot Bench

Sotomayor quickly got a reputation as a well-prepared, outspoken, intelligent, and demanding district judge. Lawyers referred to her judgeship as a hot bench, where many questions were asked, and well-prepared and organized answers were ex-

Copyright Infringement Cases

In *Tasini v. The New York Times Co.* (1997), a group of free-lance writers sued the New York Times Co. for copyright infringement, claiming its newspaper placed their articles into electronic databases without getting permission from the writers. The Times Co. argued that "they have permissibly reproduced plaintiffs' articles as part of electronic revisions of the newspapers and magazines in which those articles first appeared." Sotomayor ruled in favor of the Times Co., but the decision was reversed by the Second Circuit Court of Appeals, and the reversal was upheld by the U.S. Supreme Court.

In *Castle Rock Entertainment v. Carol Publishing Group, Inc.* (1997), the producers of the television program *Seinfeld* sued the publisher of the book *The Seinfeld Aptitude Test (SAT)* for copyright infringement. The book dealt with *Seinfeld* trivia. The publishers claimed that the book was protected under the "fair use" doctrine of the copyright act. Sotomayor ruled that the book was not protected under fair use because it took so much original material from the *Seinfeld* program that it infringed on the show's copyright. The court awarded damages and stopped the publication of the book. The Second Circuit Appeals Court upheld Sotomayor's decision.

Sonia Sotomayor, *Tasini v. The New York Times Co.*, U.S. District Court, Southern District New York, 972 F. Supp. 804, No. 93 Civ. 8678, August 13, 1997.

pected. As a panelist for the Practicing Law Institute in the early 1990s, Sotomayor explained that district judges dealt with hundreds of cases. She had some advice for attorneys: "Make your argument succinctly. Figure out what your issue is up front and don't let the judge figure it out for you. . . . If you have a weakness in your case, state it and address it. Don't attempt to hide it by skirting around it"[61]

Lauren Collins writes in the *New Yorker*, "In the courtroom, Sotomayor values preparation."[62] Criminal defense attorney Gerald Shargel told Collins, "She can be, and is, won over by lawyers who are prepared. But if a lawyer acts like a fool, she will go for the jugular."[63]

After six years as a district court judge, a seat became available on the Second Circuit Court of Appeals, and Sotomayor was again recommended by Moynihan to fill the vacancy. President Bill Clinton nominated the up-and-coming jurist on June 25, 1997, to the next higher step on the court system ladder. Senate Republicans, who disliked her liberal outlook, were fearful she was headed to the Supreme Court. They decided not to play along with the savior of baseball.

Chapter 5

The Court of Appeals: The Rule of Law in a Variety of Decisions

The U.S. Court of Appeals "hears appeals from the district courts within its circuit, as well as appeals from decisions of federal administrative agencies."[64] A judge on the Second Circuit, one of twelve circuits throughout the country, reviews cases from federal courts in New York, Connecticut, and Vermont. Antonia Felix, author of *Sonia Sotomayor: The True American Dream*, compared the appellate court to the district court on which Sotomayor had served since 1992. "The appellate court," wrote Felix, "addresses the legal points of the decision—there is no jury, no retrial, no consideration of evidence. A panel of three appellate judges reviews briefs and hears oral argument to determine whether to uphold the district court's decision. . . . Appeals judges are concerned with questions of law and public policy rather than issues of facts."[65]

The appellate courts hear a wide variety of cases ranging from First Amendment issues of free speech and religion to claims involving civil rights, criminal law, environmental law, labor law, and securities violations. In fact, the Second Circuit, according to writer John Schwartz in the *New York Times* is "the busiest appellate court for business and financial matters in the nation."[66] A seat on the Second Circuit Court of Appeals would be a challenging promotion for Sotomayor. She was an assertive jurist with strong views, who put the rule of law above her personal feelings. But her confirmation to the appeals court took much longer than she expected.

Political Maneuverings

Republican senators blocked Sotomayor's confirmation, and it took eight months for the confirmation to be approved by the Senate Judiciary Committee in March 1998. Some Republicans labeled Sotomayor as an activist judge, who made policy and did not interpret the law narrowly enough. Others did not want Clinton to be able to name the first Hispanic Supreme Court justice. Writer Neil A. Lewis of the *New York Times* quoted a senior Republican staff aide, who chose to remain anonymous,

The United States Second Circuit Court of Appeals hears cases in the Thurgood Marshall U.S. Courthouse in New York City.

For eight months after Clinton nominated Sotomayor to the Second Circuit, Republican senators blocked Sotomayor's confirmation because they feared she was an activist judge that was getting a fast track to the Supreme Court.

as stating "basically, we think that putting her on the appeals court puts her in the batter's box to be nominated to the Supreme Court."[67]

The lead editorial in the June 8, 1998, *Wall Street Journal* described what it called the "Souter Strategy" and declared that the Clinton administration wanted to "get [Sotomayor] on to the Second Circuit, then elevate her to the Supreme Court as soon as an opening occurs,"[68] which is what happened to Supreme Court justice David H. Souter. The editorial criticized some of Sotomayor's district court decisions and recommended continued delay of her confirmation. At the time of her nomination, the Supreme Court had no vacancy. Also, nothing indicated that a vacancy would open up soon, although the *Wall Street Journal* noted that perhaps Justice John Paul Stevens might soon retire, opening up a seat on the High Court. (Justice Stevens remained on the Supreme Court for twelve more years. He retired at the age of ninety in 2010).

According to Lewis, conservative talk show host Rush Limbaugh declared that Sotomayor "was an ultraliberal who was on a 'rocket ship' to the Supreme Court."[69] The Democrats were particularly annoyed with the delay because the Second Circuit, based in New York, was backlogged with cases. Hispanic organizations, including the Congressional Hispanic Caucus, lobbied and organized a petition drive to push the Senate to decide on Sotomayor. Finally, the Republican majority leader, Trent Lott of Mississippi, scheduled a Senate vote. Sotomayor was confirmed on October 2, 1998, sixteen months after her nomination by the president. In the end, she received support from twenty-five Republican senators and all the Democrats. The Supreme Court did have vacancies in 2005 and 2006, but Republican president George W. Bush nominated conservative judges John G. Roberts Jr. as chief justice and Samuel Alito as associate justice. They were both confirmed by the Senate in a timely fashion.

The Busy Second Circuit

Sotomayor was an appeals court judge on the Second Circuit for nearly eleven years, heard over three thousand cases, and wrote close to four hundred opinions. Six of her opinions were reviewed by the U.S. Supreme Court, and four were overturned. Anna C. Henning and Kenneth R. Thomas of the Congressional

Passionate About Teaching

Sotomayor worked as an adjunct professor at New York University Law School from 1997 to 2007. She was also a lecturer-in-law at Columbia University Law School from 1999 to 2009 and has been a trustee at Princeton University since 2007. Sotomayor enjoyed working with law students and gave lectures at other law schools throughout the country—from Pepperdine in California, to Syracuse University in New York, to the University of Puerto Rico. She gave talks about the Court of Appeals, discussed each step of a trial in detail, organized a moot court competition (in which law students argue imaginary cases), and even supervised students in her office as they researched and wrote about actual cases.

Research Service analyzed many of her Second Circuit opinions and concluded that

> perhaps the most consistent characteristic of Judge Sotomayor's approach as an appellate judge has been an adherence to the doctrine of stare decisis, i.e., the upholding of past judicial precedents. Other characteristics appear to include what many would describe as a careful application of particular facts at issue in a case, and a dislike for situations in which the court might be seen as overstepping its judicial role.[70]

Over the years, Judge Sotomayor wrote many notable opinions on a variety of interesting and sometimes controversial topics.

Free Speech Rights

The First Amendment to the U.S. Constitution guarantees the rights of freedom of speech, freedom of the press, freedom of religion, freedom to petition the government, and freedom of assembly without the interference of government. In *Pappas v. Giuliani* (2002), a case that dealt with free speech, the Second Circuit upheld the removal of a city employee for distributing racist materials. Thomas Pappas worked for the New York City Police Department (NYPD) in computer systems maintenance. On several occasions, he received letters from the Mineola, New York, Auxiliary Police Department asking for charitable contributions. Pappas used the reply envelopes provided and filled them with racially offensive material, which he then mailed back anonymously. The bigoted material contained slurs and statements against black people and Jews.

Pappas eventually admitted to sending the material through the mail, claiming it was a form of protest because he was tired of being asked for money. Pappas was found guilty by the NYPD in a disciplinary trial for violating a departmental regulation that prohibited the sending of "defamatory materials through the mails," and the police commissioner dismissed him from his job. Pappas sued and claimed the NYPD violated his First Amendment rights to free speech. A district court judge upheld his termination in 2000, and Pappas appealed to the Second Circuit Court of Appeals. The 2-1 panel majority held that the racist actions of Pappas, despite being anonymous and taking place during personal time at home, undermined the goals, effectiveness, and interests of the NYPD and "outweighed Pappas's interest in free speech."[71] The judgment of the district court was affirmed, but Sotomayor strongly disagreed with the majority decision.

Sotomayor upheld First Amendment freedoms despite actions that she found personally despicable. In her dissenting opinion, Sotomayor wrote,

> The Court holds that the government does not violate the First Amendment when it fires a police department employee for racially inflammatory speech—where the speech consists of mailings in which the employee did not identify himself let alone connect himself to the police department; where the speech occurred away from the office and on the employee's own time; where the employee's position involved no policymaking authority or public

contact; where there is virtually no evidence of workplace disruption resulting directly from the speech; and where it ultimately required the investigatory resources of two police departments to bring the speech to the attention of the community.[72]

Sotomayor went on to say, "I find the speech in this case patently offensive, hateful, and insulting. The Court should not, however, gloss over three decades of jurisprudence and the centrality of First Amendment freedoms in our lives because it is confronted with speech it does not like and because a government employer fears a potential public response that

Off the Bench

When she is not Judge Sotomayor, she is a typical New Yorker who goes to restaurants, the opera, the ballet, loves to shop, socialize, and entertain. She lives in a condo in Greenwich Village, has many friends, and loves the New York Yankees baseball team. *Latina Magazine* named her their Woman of the Decade, and writer Shani Saxon-Parrish noted that she was "a doting hostess . . . [who] puts together cheese platters, makes tasty salads and hooks up a mean churrasco [grilled meat with peppers and onions] with a tangy lemon marinade."[1] She also enjoys wearing fire-engine-red nail polish and semihoop black and red earrings. She is a very private person, but has accepted her status as a role model for young minority and poor children who aspire to have a better life.

Sotomayor's friend, Manhattan lawyer Dawn Cardi, told the *National Journal*, "She likes to bicycle. She likes to hike. She likes to cook. She entertains. She'll have us over for Halloween so we can see the parade from her apartment."[2] She also plays "Scattergories" every Thanksgiving with the Cardis.

Sotomayor buys more than sixty Christmas presents each year for nieces, nephews, godchildren, friends, and court staffers. Robin Kar, one of her former law clerks, told CNN.com she was a "warm, extraordinarily kind and caring it alone precipitated [brought about]."[73] Sotomayor dealt with many other cases in which freedoms guaranteed in the Bill of Rights were challenged. Each time she dealt with specific questions of law.

Unreasonable Searches and Seizures

The Fourth Amendment provides American citizens with the right to be secure and protected from unreasonable searches and seizures by government or law enforcement without probable cause

person." According to Kar, "She was the judge who, in the courthouse, for example, knew all of the doormen, knew the cafeteria workers, who knew the janitors—she didn't just know all of the other judges and the politicians. She really went out of her way to get to know everyone and was well loved by everyone."[3]

1. Shani Saxon-Parrish, "Her Honor: A Portrait of Justice Sonia Sotomayor," *Latina Magazine,* November 11, 2009. www.latina.com/lifestyle/news-politics/her-honor-portrait-justice-sonia-sotomayor.

2. *National Journal,* "Inside Washington—Some Friendly Insight," June 5, 2009.

3. "Who Is Sonia Sotomayor," CNN.com, May 26, 2009. www.cnn.com/2009/POLITICS/05/26/sotomayor.bio/index.html.

Sotomayor attends a Yankees game with nephews Conner and Corey. She is close to her extended family.

or a search warrant. In *N.G. and S.G. et al. v. State of Connecticut* (2004), Sotomayor also dissented from the majority opinion and argued against a particular method of search and seizure. In this case, the families of teenage girls in a juvenile detention facility claimed the girls were subjected to a series of strip searches in violation of their Fourth Amendment rights. The case was dismissed by the district court, and the Second Circuit upheld the right of the facility to strip search girls when they are first placed in detention to deter them from smuggling in goods that are not allowed.

Sotomayor disagreed with the majority. She wrote that "caselaw consistently has recognized the severely intrusive nature of strip searches and has placed strict limits on their use," and she quoted from an opinion of the Seventh Circuit Court of Appeals which referred to strip searches as "demeaning, dehumanizing, undignified, humiliating, terrifying, unpleasant, embarrassing, repulsive, signifying degradation and submission."[74] She opposed such general strip searches if there was no suspicion that a particular individual had smuggled goods into the detention facility.

Sotomayor declared,

> We should be especially wary of strip searches of children, since youth "is a time and condition of life when a person may be most susceptible to influence and to psychological damage." If the juvenile detention centers had performed the strip searches at issue based on reasonable individualized suspicions rooted in the dangerous tendencies of the plaintiffs, I might not question their authority to do so. . . . Reasonable suspicion must be present in order to strip search a juvenile who is not alleged to have committed a crime.[75]

Sotomayor also noted that these types of searches have not been particularly effective in the past.

Keep and Bear Arms

Gun violence was an issue with which Sotomayor was personally familiar—from the time in the late 1960s when the Bronxdale

Otis McDonald, right, speaks at a news conference with his legal team about the Supreme Court's decision to reverse Sotomayor's Second Circuit decision on the Chicago gun ban. Sotomayor, as a Supreme Court justice, dissented.

Houses began to decline into a neighborhood filled with drugs and gang activity, to her years in the district attorney's office when she prosecuted criminals. Gun and weapons ownership has been particularly controversial in America, and the Second Circuit judges heard several Second Amendment cases. The Second Amendment to the Constitution states, "A well regulated Militia, being necessary to the security of a free State, the right of the people to keep and bear Arms, shall not be infringed." In *Maloney v. Cuomo* (2009), Sotomayor was on a three-judge panel that considered a claim by James Maloney that a New York state law was unconstitutional because it prohibited the possession of nunchakus in his home. Nunchakus, which Maloney used as part of a martial arts training program, are defined as "any device designed primarily as a weapon, consisting of two or more lengths of a rigid material joined together by a thong, rope, or chain in such a manner as to allow free movement of a portion of the device while held in the hand and capable of being rotated in such a manner as to inflict serious injury upon a person by striking or choking."[76]

The district court dismissed Maloney's claim. Sotomayor and the appeals court panel agreed with the lower court and affirmed the dismissal. In her opinion Sotomayor cited the Supreme Court case of *Presser v. Illinois* (1886). In that case the Supreme Court held that the Second Amendment "is a limitation only upon the power of congress and the national government and not upon that of the state." In addition, the panel noted that nunchakus are highly dangerous weapons, and the ban against their possession is "supported by a rational basis."[77]

In *McDonald v. Chicago* (2010), the Supreme Court, in a 5-4 vote, disagreed with the Second Circuit's decision in *Maloney* and stated that the Second Amendment did apply to state and local gun control laws. By this time, Sotomayor was already on the Supreme Court and joined with justices Ruth Bader Ginsburg and Stephen Breyer in the dissenting opinion, written by justice John Paul Stevens. However, the Court upheld a state's right to impose certain restrictions on firearm possession, such as prohibiting felons and the mentally ill from owning guns, and not being allowed to carry firearms to school or in government buildings.

Cases in which whites are claiming discrimination because of their race have been increasing. The legal term for this is reverse discrimination, the opposite of the traditional discrimination experienced in America against members of minority groups. During her days on the board of directors of the Puerto Rican Legal Defense and Education Fund (PRLDEF), Sotomayor supported a traditional discrimination lawsuit against the New York City Police Department, charging their promotional exams were unfair to minority candidates. Now, as a judge, she heard a case brought by white firemen that claimed just the opposite.

Reverse Discrimination

In 2003, after administering a promotional exam to fill vacancies in the fire department of New Haven, Connecticut, city officials

The Mexico City Policy

Instituted by President Ronald Reagan in 1984, the Mexico City policy stated that the United States will not provide federal funding to nongovernmental organizations that "perform or actively promote abortion as a method of family planning."[1] The Mexico City policy was supported by President George H.W. Bush from 1988 to 1992. After it was invalidated by President Bill Clinton in 1993, President George W. Bush reinstated the Mexico City policy in 2001, but it was again rescinded by President Obama in 2009. Sotomayor wrote an opinion for the Second Circuit in *Center for Reproductive Law and Policy v. Bush* in 2002, which challenged the constitutionality of the Mexico City policy in effect at the time.

The Center for Reproductive Law and Policy argued that the government policy of withholding federal funding to organizations that performed or promoted abortions violated their First Amendment and Equal Protection rights. Sotomayor rejected the constitutional challenges and cited a prior Supreme Court case, *Planned Parenthood Federation of America v. Agency for International Development* (1990) in support of her decision. She wrote that "the Supreme Court has made clear that the government is free to favor the anti-abortion position over the pro-choice position, and can do so with public funds."[2]

1. Statement of the United States of America at the United Nations International Conference on Population (Second Session), Mexico, D.F., August 6–13, 1984. Pet. App. 4a–5a, 53a–55a.

2. *Center for Reproductive Law and Policy v. Bush*, 304 F.3d 183, U.S. Court of Appeals, Second Circuit, 2002.

found that the white candidates had much better scores than the black candidates. The top ten candidates for promotion to lieutenant were all white, and seven whites and two Hispanics were eligible for promotion to captain. Since no African Americans scored high enough to be eligible for promotion, the city scrapped the results of the exam because of the "statistical racial disparity."[78] City officials believed the test was evidence of "disparate impact," an unintentional but discriminatory effect on minorities in violation of Title VII of the 1964 Civil Rights Act, which "prohibits discrimination in employment on the basis of race, color, national origin, sex, or religion."[79] They invalidated the test results rather than be liable to a lawsuit by the minority black firefighters. As a result, the white and Hispanic firefighters sued the city of New Haven (*Ricci v. DeStefano*) for deliberate discrimination based on race, a violation of Title VII, and the Equal Protection Clause of the Fourteenth Amendment. They believed the exams were fair and impartial and that their scores, which were high enough to earn promotions, were thrown out because they were white and Hispanic.

The district court ruled in favor of the city of New Haven, and the Second Circuit Court of Appeals three-judge panel that included Sotomayor, upheld the lower court ruling. Instead of writing their own decision, the Second Circuit panel adopted the analysis and decision of the district court. The panel "issued a one paragraph unsigned opinion that . . . affirmed the district court's decision."[80] The brief summary order expressed sympathy for the white and Hispanic firefighters: "We are not unsympathetic to the plaintiffs' expression of frustration. Mr. Ricci, for example, who is dyslexic, made intensive efforts that appear to have resulted in his scoring highly on one of the exams, only to have it invalidated."[81]

The district court noted that New Haven's attempt to correct the disparate impact of the flawed promotional exam was not an intentional move to discriminate against the white and Hispanic firefighters and did not violate the Equal Protection Clause. After a request by the plaintiffs for the case to be reheard in front of the entire Second Circuit court, Sotomayor voted with the 7-6 majority against rehearing the case. One of the judges who voted to rehear the case was José Cabranes, Sotomayor's former mentor.

Ricci v. DeStefano was appealed to the Supreme Court, which reversed the lower court ruling by a 5-4 decision on June 29, 2009. The majority opinion, written by Justice Anthony Kennedy, declared, "Fear of litigation alone cannot justify an employer's reliance on race to the detriment [disadvantage] of individuals who passed the examinations and qualified for promotions. The City's discarding the test results was impermissible under Title VII."[82] In a concurring opinion, Justice Samuel Alito wrote that the city threw out the test results to please the politically important black community. The 5-4 decision indicated a strong ideological difference between the conservative majority and the liberal minority on the Supreme Court. Sotomayor's role in the Second Circuit court's decision in the *Ricci* case would come back to cause difficulty for her in the summer of 2009.

A Vacancy on the High Court

A few months after Barack Obama took office in January 2010, Charles E. Schumer and Kirsten Gillibrand, U.S. senators from New York, sent a personal letter to the White House. They strongly urged the president "to consider the Latino legal community when deciding . . . [the] first appointment to the United States Supreme Court should a vacancy occur during your presidency."[83] The two senators recommended Judge Sonia Sotomayor and Secretary of the Interior Ken Salazar as excellent candidates who would add to the diversity of the Court.

Sotomayor is introduced to the Senate by Charles Schumer and Kirsten Gillibrand. It was Schumer and Gillibrand who wrote to President Obama recommending that he appoint Sotomayor to the U.S. Supreme Court.

When Souter announced his retirement from the High Court in the spring of 2009, Sotomayor immediately turned up on the short list of names as a replacement. Obama said he was looking for "a qualified nominee with legal and real world experience, as well as an appreciation for the impact of court decisions on everyday life."[84] Although Sotomayor's friends and supporters believed she fit the bill, no one knew for sure who Obama's actual choice would be. Sotomayor was eventually told she might be getting a call from the president on May 25, so she waited in her office all day for the phone to ring. Finally she called the White House and was told the president had gotten distracted by other business and would call her that evening. They told her to go home and start packing.

At 8:10 P.M., Sotomayor's phone rang. "I had my cell phone in my right hand and I had my left hand over my chest trying to calm my beating heart. . . . The President got on the phone and said to me, 'Judge, I would like to announce you as my selection to be the next Associate Justice of the United States Supreme Court.' I caught my breath and started to cry and said, 'Thank you, Mr. President.'"[85]

Next stop for Sotomayor: the nation's capital.

Chapter 6

Nomination and Confirmation: Supreme Court Justice Sotomayor

O bama asked two promises of Sotomayor during his nomination call. "The first was to remain the person I was, and the second was to stay connected to my community," she said. "And I said to him that those were two easy promises to make, because those two things I could not change."[86]

The official White House nomination ceremony took place on May 26. It was followed by praise and celebration of the nominee, then an intense scrutiny of Sotomayor's judicial record and speeches, and public criticism by those who opposed her.

Latino Pride and Letters of Support

Sotomayor was only the second judge in history to be nominated to three different judicial positions by three different presidents—Bush, Clinton, and Obama. Her nomination sparked celebrations not only in the streets of New York City but also in Puerto Rico where cultural recognition is very important to this small island territory that belongs to the United States. According to a *New York Times* article by Damien Cave, the Puerto Rican "legislature . . . introduced three resolutions

President Barack Obama announces his nomination of Sotomayor to replace retiring justice David Souter on the U.S. Supreme Court in an East Room ceremony on May 26, 2009.

of congratulation . . . [and] . . . Miss Puerto Rico gushed that Judge Sotomayor's selection . . . proved that the island's women were not just beautiful."[87] One Puerto Rican man, Mattias Sela, told Cave, "It's a point of pride for all of us because she's risen up from the bottom. Not many of us do."[88] Another person, Juan Manuel García Passalacqua exclaimed, "This person born not of the ruling class in Puerto Rico ends up being part of the ruling class in the United States? Wow, man. This is the daughter of a nurse!"[89] Sotomayor is the highest-ranking Puerto Rican in America.

Hundreds of organizations, states, universities, cities, chambers of commerce, social workers, and law enforcement agencies wrote letters that supported Sotomayor's nomination to the Supreme Court and endorsed her confirmation by the Senate. Organizations as diverse as the National Rifle Association (NRA), the Congress of Racial Equality (CORE), the National Fraternal Order of Police, and the American Association of People with

Disabilities wrote glowing letters to the Judiciary Committee of the U.S. Senate.

The Women's Bar Association of the State of New York (WBASNY), of which Sotomayor is a member, wrote, "While always adhering to established law and precedent, her opinions and decisions reveal a special sensitivity to challenges facing those whom WBASNY seeks to protect: women and other groups for whom the equal administration of justice has been elusive, such as immigrants, children, and the disabled."[90] Not all comments about Sotomayor were praiseworthy and supportive. A remark taken from a past speech was examined, analyzed, and criticized by the media and the conservative opposition.

1994 Remark Raises Controversy

Sotomayor made a speech to the Conference on Law Reviews on March 17, 1994. She talked about gender and the law, and quoted a remark from Supreme Court justice Sandra Day O'Connor (now retired) that "a wise old man and a wise old woman reach the same conclusion."[91] Sotomayor disagreed with O'Connor and stated, "I would hope that a wise woman with the richness of her experience would, more often than not, reach a better conclusion. What is better? I . . . hope that better will mean a more compassionate and caring conclusion."[92] Similar remarks were made by Sotomayor in speeches throughout the 1990s.

Sotomayor's nomination sparked celebrations and massive support from the New York Latino community and Puerto Rico.

In 2001 she made several changes to that remark in a speech at the University of California at Berkeley School of Law, admitting that both gender and ethnicity may influence a judge's decision. In the speech titled, "A Latina Woman's Voice," Sotomayor said, "Justice O'Connor has often been cited as saying that a wise old man and a wise old woman will reach the same conclusion in deciding cases. . . . I would hope that a wise Latina woman with the richness of her experience would more often than not reach a better conclusion than a white male who hasn't lived that life."[93]

These remarks were included in speeches given by Sotomayor into 2003. At the time, they were not controversial nor were they brought up at her confirmation hearings in 1992 or 1998. It was not until she was nominated to the Supreme Court in 2009 that Sotomayor's opponents quoted lines from these speeches and expressed concerns about racism.

Does Life Experience Equal Bias?

Writer Dana Milbank wrote in the *Washington Post* that an hour before her nomination, Fox News anchors and guests began to discuss Sotomayor's "wise Latina" comment with phrases like "reverse racism . . . revolutionary, radical . . . completely counter to the notion that justice should be blind."[94] Conservative Republican and former Speaker of the House Newt Gingrich wrote on Twitter, "Imagine a judicial nominee said, 'my experience as a white man makes me better than a Latina woman.'. . . White man racist nominee would be forced to withdraw, Latina woman racist should also withdraw."[95] Conservative author and commentator Ann Coulter stated, "Saying that someone would decide a case differently . . . because she's a Latina, not a white male. That statement by definition is racist."[96]

According to FoxNews.com, Republican senators called Sotomayor's remark "troubling" but stated that the term "racist . . . [was] off limits and should not be used to describe an accomplished and respected jurist."[97] A few days later, Gingrich said that his words were "perhaps too strong and direct." He admitted that her judicial rulings have "shown more caution and

Sotomayor explains her "wise Latina" comment to Republican senators during her Senate confirmation hearings.

moderation" than her speeches, but he stated the wise Latina comments "reveal a betrayal of a fundamental principle of the American system—that everyone is equal before the law."[98]

Senator Chuck Schumer, Democrat from New York, declared on *This Week*, the television program on ABC, "As long as you put rule of law first, of course, it's quite natural to understand that our experiences affect us."[99] Schumer added, "The specific sentence there is simply saying that people's experiences matter and we ought to have some diversity of experience on the court."[100]

Her Speeches Differ from Her Record

Generally, Sotomayor's speeches during the seventeen years she has served on the bench were more representative of her identification as a Puerto Rican and a woman. But an analysis of her judicial record showed she has been an impartial judge for whom the law came first. Sotomayor said that like everyone else,

Modest Financial Assets

Several millionaires are on the Supreme Court, but Sotomayor is not one of them. Ginsburg is the wealthiest, with assets, according to the *New York Times*, of "as much as $45 million." Other millionaires on the High Court include Roberts., Breyer, Scalia, Stevens, and Kagan.

Sotomayor's modest assets are the lowest of the justices, and she and Scalia were the only members of the Court to list liabilities [debts]. She owes money to credit card companies and for dental work like many other Americans. She has refinanced the mortgage several times on her two-bedroom condominium in Greenwich Village, New York, and helps support her elderly mother and her mother's husband in Florida.

Associate justices of the Supreme Court have a salary of $213,900 per year. After the age of sixty-five, all members of the Court receive a yearly pension equal to their salary, once they retire.

New York Times, "Supreme Court Runs Financial Gamut,"June 11, 2010. www.nytimes.com/2010/06/12/us/12scotus.html.

Sotomayor's modest assets include her Greenwich Village condominium.

she has been influenced to a certain extent by her background and upbringing. Even conservative justice Samuel Alito made similar comments during his confirmation hearings. Alito said, "When I get a case about discrimination, I have to think about people in my own family who suffered discrimination because of their ethnic background or because of religion or because of gender. And I do take that into account."[101] No one on the panel questioned his statement.

After she was nominated to sit on the High Court, conservatives and some Republican critics expressed concern that Sotomayor was an activist liberal judge, yet a study of her record shows the opposite. Writers Steve LeVine and Theo Francis note in *BusinessWeek Online* that Sotomayor has been more of a moderate on important business issues. *Wall Street Journal* writers Jess Bravin and Nathan Koppel stated that Sotomayor's criminal rulings sometimes agreed with the High Court's top conservative justices, most likely because of her time as a prosecutor working with law enforcement. New York defense lawyer Michael Bachner told Bravin and Koppel that Sotomayor "can be 'very tough' on white-collar defendants from privileged backgrounds, but is 'more understanding of individuals who grew up in a tougher circumstance.'"[102] Jeffrey Rosen writes in *Time* that in her "226 published majority opinions and 19 dissenting opinions, Sotomayor has tilted toward the left [liberal] on immigration and gender cases but sided with conservatives on criminal matters."[103]

Ricci Revisited: Reverse Discrimination

The Supreme Court overruled the Second Circuit panel that included Sotomayor in *Ricci v. DeStefano* just weeks before the Senate confirmation hearings were to begin. After the Supreme Court reversal, two Republicans members of the Senate Judiciary Committee made statements critical of Sotomayor. Senator John Cornyn of Texas said, "All nine justices were critical of the trial court opinion that Judge Sotomayor endorsed."[104] Senator Jeff Sessions of Alabama declared, "The Supreme Court found that Judge Sotomayor was wrong to allow the city to change its promotion exam after it was given, solely to favor a group because of race."[105]

Supporters of Sotomayor reminded critics that she was only one of a three-judge panel; she was not the senior judge hearing the case, and the short opinion in *Ricci* followed Second Circuit standards. At issue was whether the promotional exam was "race neutral." The white firefighters felt the exam was, but the city of New Haven, as evidenced by the lack of African Americans eligible for promotion, believed the test was not race neutral. (Although nine African American candidates did pass the exam, none scored high enough to qualify for a promotion).

As Sotomayor approached the confirmation hearings in the summer of 2009, she knew the Republicans on the Senate Judiciary Committee would question her extensively on her "wise Latina" comment and *Ricci v. Stefano*, among other things. But the Democrats had a comfortable majority in the Senate, and her confirmation was all but assured unless she made a terrible mistake under heated questioning. The only real question was: How many Republicans would vote for her?

Cool Under Pressure

The confirmation hearings took place during the week of July 13, 2009, in Room 216 of the Hart Senate Office Building in Washington, D.C. Sotomayor sat alone facing the nineteen members of the Judiciary Committee who were seated around her on three sides. She had a yellow legal pad on the desk, writing instruments to take notes, and two filled glasses. One held water, while the other held Sprite, to keep her blood sugar at the proper level.

It was not long before Sessions, the top Republican on the committee, questioned Sotomayor about her "wise Latina" comment. "I am very troubled," he said, "that you would repeatedly over a decade or more make [such] statements."[106] Other Republicans followed with similar criticism, and Sotomayor responded that her remark was "a rhetorical flourish that fell flat." She explained that the comment "was bad, because it left an impression that I believed that life experiences commanded a result in a case." She was trying "to inspire young Hispanics, Latino students and lawyers to believe that their life experiences added value to the process."[107]

Making Her Views Known

Sotomayor used the confirmation hearings to clarify past statements and explain her opinions. She stated, "It is very clear that I don't base my judgments on my personal experiences—or my feelings or my biases."[108] She went on to stress that "judges can't rely on what's in their heart. They don't determine the law. Congress makes the laws. The job of a judge is to apply the law."[109]

Sotomayor declared, "My record shows that at no point or time have I ever permitted my personal views or sympathies

Alabama senator Jeff Sessions tried to paint Sotomayor as a judicial activist even though evidence to support the accusation was never found.

to influence the outcome of a case. . . . I want to state upfront, unequivocally and without doubt: I do not believe that any racial, ethnic or gender group has an advantage in sound judging. I do believe that every person has an equal opportunity to be a good and wise judge, regardless of their background or life experiences."[110]

In response to *Ricci v. DeStefano*, Sotomayor said that she and her fellow judges on the panel decided that case on the basis of the district court decision and established precedent. On gun and weapons control, Sotomayor stated she also followed Supreme Court precedent, and on abortion she believed the Supreme Court's decision in *Roe v. Wade*, which legalized abortion in 1973, was settled law.

Sotomayor answered all questions at the confirmation hearings, no matter how critical, in a calm and deliberate manner. She was confident and friendly with both Republicans and Democrats and exhibited a warm sense of humor. It was not surprising that on July 28, 2009, the Senate Judiciary Committee approved her nomination 13 to 6. On August 6, 2009, the full Senate voted 68 to 31 in support of her confirmation. Republicans accounted for 9 of the 68 affirmative votes.

Associate Justice of the Supreme Court

Sotomayor became the 111th justice to sit on the High Court, the first Hispanic, the third woman, and the only sitting justice to have served on a trial court. She was also the third New Yorker on the High Court. Justice Elena Kagan, who replaced Stevens in 2010, was the fourth New Yorker on the Court. Sotomayor grew up in the Bronx, Ginsburg is from Brooklyn, Scalia grew up in Queens, and Kagan is from Manhattan, all boroughs of New York City.

The Supreme Court term that began on October 5, 2009, the first Monday of that month, included a five-member conservative majority—Chief Justice John G. Roberts Jr. and justices Antonin Scalia, Clarence Thomas, Samuel Alito, and Anthony Kennedy.

Sotomayor, as her brother Juan Luis looks on and her mother Celina holds the Bible, takes the oath for associate justice of the Supreme Court from chief justice John Roberts on August 8, 2009.

Sotomayor was part of a four-member liberal minority, along with Justices Ruth Bader Ginsburg, Stephen Breyer, and John Paul Stevens. Kennedy has sometimes acted as the swing vote between the conservative and liberal groups. A little over two months after joining the Court, Sotomayor wrote her first official opinion.

A tradition at the Supreme Court is that a new justice's first written opinion be based on a unanimous decision. The Court ruled 9-0 in the case of *Mohawk Industries v. Carpenter* (2009), and Sotomayor, the newest member of the Court, read the opinion out loud on December 8, 2009. The case involved an employee of Mohawk Industries, Norman Carpenter, who filed suit in federal court in Georgia claiming he was wrong-

Constitutional Guarantee to Freedom of Religion

Justices Sotomayor and Ginsburg joined in a dissent written by Justice Stevens in *Salazar v. Buono* (2010). A five-foot cross in the Mojave Desert National Preserve in California was designated as a national memorial to veterans of World War I. A lawsuit claimed that putting the cross on federal property violated the Establishment Clause of the First Amendment, which deals with the constitutional guarantee of freedom of religion and the separation of church and state. Both the federal district court and the Ninth Circuit Court of Appeals ruled that the placement of a religious symbol on federal property was a constitutional violation.

To overcome this ruling, the U.S. Congress then passed a law that swapped that federal property for another nearby parcel of land. The land on which the cross stood then became private property, and the cross remained in place. The Supreme Court in *Salazar v. Buono* (in another 5-4 decision), reversed the lower court decisions and approved Congress's land-swap statute. In a dissent, Stevens wrote that Congress was endorsing a particular religious message by allowing the cross to remain. He noted that the government should honor all veterans, regardless of their faith, and that the government's constitutional responsibility was to avoid support for a particular religious view.

fully terminated. Carpenter requested documents that Mohawk believed were protected by attorney-client privilege. The district court ruled in favor of Carpenter, but the Eleventh Circuit Court of Appeals dismissed the case. The Supreme Court unanimously upheld the decision of the appeals court.

When there is an ideological split on the High Court, Sotomayor has often voted with the other liberal members, although that is not always the case.

Votes Liberal with Exceptions

Sotomayor sided with conservative members of the Court in the case of an Alabama man who had been sentenced to death in *Wood v. Allen* (2010). Wood claimed that he had ineffective counsel because his lawyer failed to tell the court that he was mentally deficient at his sentencing hearing. The federal district court ruled in Wood's favor, but the U.S. Court of Appeals for the Eleventh Circuit reversed the lower court decision. Sotomayor, in a 7-2 majority opinion that affirmed the Eleventh Circuit ruling, wrote that Wood's attorney made a strategic decision not to present evidence of his mental deficiencies, and it was not unreasonable.

Sotomayor again joined with the majority of the Court in the combined case of *Graham v. Florida* and *Sullivan v. Florida* (2010). The Court ruled that it was cruel and unusual punishment, under the Eighth Amendment, to give a life prison term without possibility of parole to a convicted offender who is a juvenile and did not murder anyone. At the time of their sentencing, Sullivan was thirteen years old and Graham was seventeen years old. One of the most publicized cases since Sotomayor has been on the Court involved a narrowing of Miranda rights protection.

Miranda Rights

In *Miranda v. Arizona* (1966) the Supreme Court ruled that criminal suspects must be informed of their constitutional right against self-incrimination (Fifth Amendment) and the right to an attorney (Sixth Amendment) before any police questioning. That means a suspect who is arrested must be informed that he or she has the right to remain silent and that anything said can be used in court against him or her. The suspect must also be told he or she has the right to an attorney. If the suspect indicates he or she wants to remain silent, police questioning must stop. If he or she wants an attorney, questioning must stop and the suspect must be allowed to talk with the attorney. Any statements made by suspects once they have been arrested, but before they have been informed of their Miranda rights, may be ruled inadmissible in court, and that includes a confession. A Miranda rights case came before the Supreme Court in 2010, and Sotomayor wrote a dissenting opinion in which Stevens, Ginsburg, and Breyer joined.

Speak Up to Remain Silent

Van Chester Thompkins was arrested in 2001 for shooting and killing Samuel Morris the year before, outside a Michigan mall. He was read his Miranda rights and, according to a *New York Times* article by writer Adam Liptak, "refused to sign a form acknowledging that he understood them."

> Mr. Thompkins then remained almost entirely silent in the face of three hours of interrogation though he did say that his chair was hard and that he did not want a peppermint. After two hours and 45 minutes of questioning, Mr. Thompkins said yes in response to each of three questions: 'Do you believe in God?' 'Do you pray to God?' And, crucially, 'Do you pray to God to forgive you for shooting that boy down?' His affirmative response to the last question was used against him at trial, and he was convicted of first-degree murder."[111]

Thompkins was sentenced to life in prison without parole, and he appealed.

The question before the High Court in *Berghuis v. Thompkins* was: Did Thompkins waive his right to remain silent by answering "yes" to those last few questions, despite the fact that he had remained silent for nearly three hours? The state courts and the federal district court ruled that he had waived his right to remain silent. The Sixth Circuit Court of Appeals reversed the district court, and the Supreme Court in a 5-4 conservative/liberal split decision reversed the Sixth Circuit.

Writing for the majority, Kennedy noted that "the fact that the defendant [Thompkins] was silent during [the] first two hours and 45 minutes of [the] three hour interrogation was insufficient to invoke his right to remain silent under Miranda; defendant waived his right to remain silent . . . by responding to [a] question by [the] interrogating officer; police are not required to obtain a waiver of defendant's right to remain silent . . . before commencing interrogation."[112]

Weakening of Miranda Protections

In her dissenting opinion, Sotomayor wrote: "[A] heavy burden rests on the government to demonstrate that the defendant knowingly and intelligently waived his privilege against self-incrimination and his right to retained or appointed counsel. . . . That Thompkins did not make the . . . statements at issue until after approximately 2 hours and 45 minutes of interrogation serves as 'strong evidence' against waiver."[113]

Sotomayor added, "I cannot agree with the Court's much broader ruling that a suspect must clearly invoke his right to silence by speaking. [The decision] . . . invites police to question a suspect at length—notwithstanding his persistent refusal to answer questions—in the hope of eventually obtaining a single . . . response which will suffice to prove waiver of rights."[114] Sotomayor noted that advising suspects of their Miranda rights does not explain that they must speak up to protect those rights. She suggested that the police clarify the issue by asking the suspect if he or she wants to talk or wants an attorney.

"[This] . . . decision turns Miranda upside down," declared Sotomayor. "Criminal suspects must now . . . invoke their right to remain silent—which . . . requires them to speak. At the same time, suspects will be legally presumed to have waived their rights even if they have given no clear expression of their intent to do so."[115]

A Bright Future

On June 4, 2010, Sotomayor returned to the Bronx to deliver a commencement address at Eugenio Maria de Hostos Community College. Hostos is the City University of New York's first and only bilingual college, where Celina Sotomayor graduated from the nursing program in 1973. Celina accompanied her daughter to hear the class valedictorian, Melissa Diaz, say that whenever she needs inspiration, she looks to Sonia Sotomayor, a local girl who made good.

The 350 graduates and their families listened closely as Sotomayor spoke:

As you all know, our family is a lot like your family. We come from the same background, we have lived many of

Supreme Court Demographics

With the confirmation of Elena Kagan in 2010, three women are now sitting on the U.S. Supreme Court for the first time. Considering that females make up 50.7 percent of the population as of 2008, many argue that the High Court should have another female member if it is to look more like America. The addition of Sotomayor, who is Catholic, and Kagan, who is Jewish, means the Court is composed of six Catholics (Antonin Scalia, Samuel Alito, John G. Roberts Jr., Anthony Kennedy, Clarence Thomas, and Sonia Sotomayor) and three Jewish Justices (Stephen Breyer, Ruth Bader Ginsburg, and Elena Kagan). Not a single Protestant is on the Court in a nation that is about 50 percent Protestant. About 25 percent of Americans are Catholic, and less than 2 percent are Jewish. Does religion matter? Technically, the personal views of a Supreme Court justice are outweighed by the application of the law. But some issues such as abortion and the death penalty may be linked to religious beliefs. Whether justices can completely put aside personal beliefs and apply the law impartially remains to be seen.

The justices' educational backgrounds place them among the elite of society, leading some to question whether the Court is a fair representation of American society. No member of the Supreme Court has ever attended a state university. All graduated from Ivy League law schools—five from Harvard (Kennedy, Roberts, Scalia, Breyer, and Kagan), three from Yale (Thomas, Alito, and Sotomayor), and one from Columbia (Ginsburg).

The 2011 U.S Supreme Court consists of (front row, left to right) Associate Justice Clarence Thomas, Associate Justice Antonin Scalia, Chief Justice John G. Roberts, Associate Justice Anthony M. Kennedy, Associate Justice Ruth Bader Ginsburg, (back row, left to right) Associate Justice Sonia Sotomayor, Associate Justice Stephen Breyer, Associate Justice Samuel Alito Jr., and Associate Justice Elena Kagan.

the same struggles and we have faced many of the same challenges that you have faced. All of you who have come from a foreign land in this audience, all of you who are the first college graduates in your families, all of you who have struggled so hard to get where you are, you are living proof, like my brother and I, that we can make it.[116]

That same day, the Bronxdale Houses and Community Center was renamed the Justice Sonia Sotomayor Houses and Community Center by the New York City Housing Authority. It was the first time a city development was named for a living former resident.

Sotomayor has accomplished much in her lifetime, climbing her way from a Bronx housing project to the Supreme Court of the United States. But much more to this story of an American dream coming true will unfold as she helps to interpret and apply the laws of the land and the Constitution for decades to come.

Introduction: Pursuing the Dream

1. Sonia Sotomayor, "Remarks by Judge Sonia Sotomayor and the President in Nominating Judge Sonia Sotomayor to the United States Supreme Court," press release, Office of the Press Secretary, White House, May 26, 2009.
2. Barack Obama, in "Remarks by Judge Sonia Sotomayor and the President."
3. Quoted in Greg B. Smith, "Judge's Journey to Top: Bronx' Sotomayor Rose from Projects to Court of Appeals," *New York Daily News*, October 24, 1998.
4. Sonia Sotomayor, interview, *Visiones*, PBS, video, *New York Times* Video Library, 2009. http://video.nytimes.com/video/2009/06/10/us/politics/1194840839325/interview-on-visiones.html.
5. Quoted in Stuart Taylor Jr., "Commentary—Grading Sotomayor's Senior Thesis," *National Journal*, June 2, 2009.
6. Quoted in Smith, "Judge's Journey to Top."
7. Quoted in Office of the Press Secretary, "Judge Sonia Sotomayor," White House, May 26. 2009. www.whitehouse.gov/the_press_office/Background-on-Judge-Sonia-Sotomayor.

Chapter 1: The Early Years: Overcoming Adversity

8. Jonah Winter, *A Judge Grows in the Bronx*. New York: Atheneum, 2009.
9. Sonia Sotomayor, "A Latina Judge's Voice," address to the "Raising the Bar" symposium at the UC Berkeley School of Law, October 26, 2001. www.berkeley.edu/news/media/releases/2009/05/26_sotomayor.shtml.
10. Sonia Sotomayor, "Induction to a 'Wall of Fame,'" speech delivered at Bronx Community Health Center, New York, September 2007, *New York Times* Video Library. http://video.ny

times.com/video/2009/06/10/us/politics/1194840835085/
induction-to-a-wall-of-fame.html.

11. Sotomayor, "Induction to a 'Wall of Fame.'"

12. Quoted in Scott Shane and Manny Fernandez, "A Judge's Own Story Highlights Her Mother's," *New York Times*, May 28, 2009. www.nytimes.com/2009/05/28/us/ politics/28mother.html?pagewanted=print.

13. Nancy Drew Sleuth Unofficial Website, "The History of Nancy Drew." www.nancydrewsleuth.com/history.html.

14. Sonia Sotomayor, address at Stamford Middle School, Stamford, Connecticut, Fall 2004, *New York Times* Video Library. http://video.nytimes.com/video/2009/06/10/us/ politics/1194840835207/address-at-stamford-middle-school.html.

15. Sotomayor, "Induction to a 'Wall of Fame.'"

16. Sotomayor, "Induction to a 'Wall of Fame.'"

17. Sotomayor, "Induction to a 'Wall of Fame.'"

18. Sotomayor, "A Latina Judge's Voice."

19. Sotomayor, "A Latina Judge's Voice."

20. Sotomayor, "Induction to a 'Wall of Fame.'"

21. Robin Shulman, "Supreme Change," *Washington Post*, June 16, 2009.

22. Shulman, "Supreme Change."

23. Quoted in Shane and Fernandez, "A Judge's Own Story Highlights Her Mother's."

24. Quoted in Lisa Lucus and David Saltonstall, "Sonia Sotomayor's Mother Tells News: I Overcame Odds to Raise U.S. Supreme Court Pick," *New York Daily News*, May 28, 2009.

Chapter 2: Academic Activist: Rediscovering Her Roots

25. Quoted in Jennifer Ludden and Linton Weeks, "Sotomayor: 'Always Looking over My Shoulder,'" National Public Radio, May 26, 2009. www.npr.org/templates/story/story .php?storyId=104538436.

26. Quoted in Elizabeth Landau, "Cricket, Ivy League Classmates Startled Student Sonia Sotomayor," CNN.com,

July 15, 2009. www.cnn.com/2009/US/07/15/sotomayor
.college/index.html.

27. Jodi Kantor and David Gonzalez, "For Sotomayor and Thomas, Paths Diverge at Race," *New York Times*, June 7, 2009. www.nytimes.com/2009/06/07/us/politics/07affirm .html?pagewanted=print.

28. Quoted in Evan Thomas, Stuart Taylor Jr., and Brian No, "Meet the Sotomayors," *Newsweek*, July 20, 2009.

29. Sonia Sotomayor, "Anti-Latino Discrimination at Princeton," *Daily Princetonian*, May 27, 2009. www.dailyprince tonian.com/2009/05/27/23731.

30. Sotomayor, "Anti-Latino Discrimination at Princeton."

31. Quoted in David Leimer, "Latin Student Groups Assail University Hiring Performance," *Daily Princetonian*, April 22, 1974.

32. Thomas, Taylor, and No, "Meet the Sotomayors."

33. Quoted in Thomas, Taylor, and No, "Meet the Sotomayors."

34. Peter Nicholas and James Oliphant, "Two Sides to Sonia Sotomayor," *Los Angeles Times*, May 31, 2009. www.la times.com.

35. Amy Goldstein, "A Steady Rise, Punctuated by Doubts," *Washington Post*, July 12, 2009. www.washingtonpost.com/ wp-dyn/content/article/2009/07/11/AR2009071102788_ pf.html.

Chapter 3: Criminal Law, Civil Law, and Public Service: Gaining Experience

36. Benjamin Weiser and William K. Rashbaum, "Sotomayor Is Recalled as a Driven Rookie Prosecutor," *New York Times*, June 8, 2009. www.nytimes.com/2009/06/08/us/ politics/08prosecutor.html?pagewanted=print.

37. *New York Times Magazine*, "Robert M. Morgenthau," January 1, 2010. http://topics.nytimes.com/top/reference/ timestopics/people/m/robert_m_morgenthau/index.html.

38. Quoted in Jonathan Barzilay, "The D.A.'s Right Arms," *New York Times*, November 27, 1983. www.nytimes .com/1983/11/27/magazine/the-da-s-right-arms.html.

39. Quoted in Ann O'Neill, "Sotomayor Learned the Ropes on 'Tarzan' Case," CNN.com, July 16, 2009. www.cnn

.com/2009/US/07/16/sotomayor.district.attorney/index.html.

40. Dina Temple-Raston, "Sotomayor's Real-World Schooling in Law and Order," National Public Radio, June 9, 2009. www.npr.org/templates/story/story.php?storyID=105005007.

41. Quoted in Temple-Raston, "Sotomayor's Real-World Schooling in Law and Order."

42. Quoted in Barzilay, "The D.A.'s Right Arms."

43. Quoted in Weiser and Rashbaum, "Sotomayor Is Recalled as a Driven Rookie Prosecutor."

44. Quoted in Amy Goldstein and Alec MacGillis, "Sotomayor Was a Passionate but Civil Activist," *Washington Post*, June 1, 2009. www.washingtonpost.com/wp-dyn/content/article/2009/05/31/AR2009053101935_pf.html.

45. Sonia Sotomayor, "Facing the 90s as a Woman Lawyer," Practicing Law Institute panelist, early 1990s, *New York Times* Video Library. http://video.nytimes.com/video/2009/06/10/us/politics/1194840834851/practicing-law-institute-panelist.html.

46. Charlie Savage and Michael Powell, "In New York, Sotomayor Put Focus on the Poor," *New York Times*, June 19, 2009. www.nytimes.com/2009/06/19/us/19mortgage.html?pagewanted=print.

47. Quoted in Savage and Powell, "In New York, Sotomayor Put Focus on the Poor."

48. Savage and Powell, "In New York, Sotomayor Put Focus on the Poor."

49. Charlie Savage, "A Long Record on Campaign Finance, Often in Support of Regulations," *New York Times*, May 30, 2009. www.nytimes.com/2009/05/30/us/politics/30judge.html?pagewanted=print.

50. Goldstein, "A Steady Rise, Punctuated by Doubts," July 12, 2009.

Chapter 4: Federal Judgeship: The Savior of Baseball

51. Quoted in Leonidas Ralph Mecham, "Understanding the Federal Courts," Administrative Office of the U.S. Courts, Office of Judges Programs, Washington, D.C., 2003.

52. David Cone, "Former MLB Pitcher David Cone Testifies at Sonia Sotomayor's Confirmation Hearings," Congressional Quarterly Transcriptions, *Washington Post*, July 16, 2009. www.washingtonpost.com/wp-dyn/content/article/2009/07/16/AR2009071603651_pf.html.
53. Cone, "Former MLB Pitcher David Cone Testifies at Sonia Sotomayor's Confirmation Hearings."
54. Sonia Sotomayor, *Silverman v. Major League Baseball Players Relations Committee, Inc.* No. 95 Civ. 2054, U.S. District Court, Southern District New York, April 3, 1995.
55. Sotomayor, *Silverman v. Major League Baseball.*
56. Cone, "Former MLB Pitcher David Cone Testifies at Sonia Sotomayor's Confirmation Hearings."
57. Sonia Sotomayor, *Flamer v. City of White Plains, New York*, 841 F. Supp. 1367, U.S. District Court, Southern District New York, December 6, 1993.
58. Sotomayor, *Flamer v. City of White Plains.*
59. Quoted in Queenie Wong, "Sonia Sotomayor's 13 Most Notable Decisions," *U.S. News and World Report*, August 6, 2009. www.usnews.com/listings/sonia-sotomayor-decisions/13-campos-v-coughlin.
60. Quoted in Wong, "Sonia Sotomayor's 13 Most Notable Decisions."
61. Sotomayor, "Facing the 90s as a Woman Lawyer."
62. Lauren Collins, "Number Nine," *New Yorker*, January 11, 010. www.newyorker.com/reporting/2010/01/11/100 111fa_fact_collins?printable=true.
63. Quoted in Collins, "Number Nine."

Chapter 5: The Court of Appeals: The Rule of Law in a Variety of Decisions

64. Quoted in Mecham, "Understanding the Federal Courts," 2003.
65. Antonia Felix, *Sonia Sotomayor: The True American Dream.* New York: Berkley, 2010, p. 188.
66. John Schwartz, "Sotomayor's Appellate Opinions Are Unpredictable, Lawyers and Schools Say," *New York Times*, May 28, 2009. www.nytimes.com/2009/05/28/us/politics/28circuit.html?pagewanted=print.

67. Quoted in Neil A. Lewis, "G.O.P., Its Eyes on High Court, Blocks a Judge," *New York Times*, June 13, 1998.
68. *Wall Street Journal*, "The Souter Strategy," editorial, June 8, 1998.
69. Lewis, "G.O.P., Its Eyes on High Court, Blocks a Judge."
70. Anna C. Henning and Kenneth R. Thomas, "Judge Sonia Sotomayor: Analysis of Selected Opinions," Congressional Research Service, June 19, 2009.
71. Quoted in *Pappas v. Giuliani*, 290 F.3d 143, U.S. Court of Appeals, Second Circuit, 2002.
72. Sonia Sotomayor, *Pappas v. Giuliani*, dissenting opinion, 290 F.3d 143, U.S. Court of Appeals, Second Circuit, 2002.
73. Sotomayor, *Pappas v. Giuliani*, 2002.
74. Sonia Sotomayor, *N.G. and S.G. et al. v. State of Connecticut*, dissenting opinion, 382 F.3d 225, U.S. Court of Appeals, Second Circuit, 2004.
75. Sotomayor, *N.G. and S.G. et al. v. State of Connecticut*, 2004.
76. Quoted in *Maloney v. Cuomo*, 554 F.3d 56, U.S. Court of Appeals, Second Circuit, 2009.
77. Quoted in *Maloney v. Cuomo*, 2009.
78. Anthony Kennedy, *Ricci v. DeStefano*, 557 U.S. (2009).
79. Civil Rights Act, Title VII, 1964, 42 U.S.C. § 2000e-2.
80. Henning and Thomas, "Judge Sonia Sotomayor: Analysis," Congressional Research Service, 2009.
81. Quoted in Adam Liptak, "New Scrutiny of Judge's Most Controversial Case," *New York Times*, June 6, 2009. www.nytimes.com/2009/06/06/us/politics/06ricci.html?pagewanted=print.
82. Kennedy, *Ricci v. DeStefano*.
83. Charles Schumer and Kirsten Gillibrand, "Schumer, Gillibrand Make Direct Appeal to President Obama, Recommending He Nominate the First Ever Latino to the Supreme Court," text of Senators' letter to President Obama, press release. http://schumer.senate.gov/new_website/record_print.cfm?id=311344.
84. Quoted in Keith B. Richburg, "N.Y. Federal Judge Likely on Shortlist," *Washington Post*, May 7, 2009. www.wash

ingtonpost.com/wp-dyn/content/article/2009/05/06/
AR2009050603762_pf.html.

85. Sonia Sotomayor, interview by C-Span. www.c-span.org/
Watch/Media/2009/09/25/HP/R/23538/Justice+Sotomayor
+On+The+Call+From+President+Obama.aspx.

Chapter 6: Nomination and Confirmation: Supreme Court Justice Sotomayor

86. Sotomayor, interview by C-Span.

87. Damien Cave, "In Puerto Rico, Supreme Court Pick with Island Roots Becomes a Superstar," *New York Times,* May 30, 2009.

88. Quoted in Cave, "In Puerto Rico, Supreme Court Pick with Island Roots Becomes a Superstar."

89. Quoted in Cave, "In Puerto Rico, Supreme Court Pick with Island Roots Becomes a Superstar."

90. Women's Bar Association of the State of New York, "Statement in Support of Judge Sonia Sotomayor," U.S. Senate Committee on the Judiciary, June 30, 2009. http://judiciary .senate.gov/nominations/SupremeCourt/SotomayorIndex .cfm#QFRs.

91. Quoted in Ted Barrett and Dana Bash, "Sotomayor Backers Cite 1994 Speech," CNN.com, June 3, 2009. www.cnn .com/2009/POLITICS/06/03/sotomayor.supporters .speech/index.html.

92. Quoted in Barrett and Bash, "Sotomayor Backers Cite 1994 Speech."

93. Sotomayor, "A Latina Judge's Voice."

94. Quoted in Dana Milbank, "Latina Woman, Tongue-Tied Man," *Washington Post,* May 28, 2009. www.wash ingtonpost.com/wp-dyn/content/article/2009/05/27/ AR2009052703323_pf.html.

95. Quoted in *Daily News* Staff, "GOP Holy Trinity on Supreme Court Nominee Sonia Sotomayor: She's a 'Racist,' *NY Daily News,* May 28, 2009.

96. Quoted in *Daily News* Staff, "GOP Holy Trinity on Supreme Court Nominee Sonia Sotomayor."

97. Quoted in FoxNews.com, "Republicans Begin to Find Voice on Racial Aspects of Sotomayor Nomination," May 31, 2009.

98. Quoted in Julie Hirschfeld Davis, "Gingrich Backtracks on Calling Sotomayor a Racist," *Dallas Morning News*, June 4, 2009.

99. FoxNews.com, "Republicans Begin to Find Voice on Racial Aspects of Sotomayor Nomination."

100. Quoted in Kenneth P. Vogel and Josh Gerstein, "Dems Differ on 'Wise Latina' Defenses," POLITICO, May 31, 2009. http://dyn.politico.com/printstory.cfm?uuid=986813F0-18FE-70B2-A8DE70481E99E127.

101. Quoted in *New York Times*, editorial, May 30, 2009.

102. Quoted in Jess Bravin and Nathan Koppel, "Nominee's Criminal Rulings Tilt to Right of Souter," *Wall Street Journal*, June 5, 2009. http://online.wsj.com/article/SB124415867263187033.html.

103. Jeffrey Rosen, "Where She Really Stands on Race," *Time*, June 22, 2009.

104. Quoted in James Vicini, "Update 3—US Court Overrules Obama Nominee in Race Bias Case," Reuters, June 29, 2009. www.reuters.com/assets/print?aid=USN2936044120090629.

105. Quoted in Vicini, "Update 3."

106. Quoted in msnbc.com, "Sotomayor Pushes Back on GOP's Bias Claim," July 14, 2009. www.msnbc.msn.com/id/31904261/print/1/displaymode/1098.

107. Quoted in Amy Goldstein, Robert Barnes, and Paul Kane, "Sotomayor Emphasizes Objectivity," *Washington Post*, July 15, 2009. www.washingtonpost.com/wp-dyn/content/article/2009/07/14/AR2009071400992_pf.html.

108. Quoted in Goldstein, Barnes, and Kane, "Sotomayor Emphasizes Objectivity."

109. Quoted in msnbc.com, "Sotomayor Pushes Back on GOP's Bias Claim."

110. Quoted in msnbc.com, "Sotomayor Pushes Back on GOP's Bias Claim."

111. Adam Liptak, "You Have the Right to Remain Silent. But Don't If You Want to Use It," *New York Times*, June 2, 2010.
112. Anthony Kennedy, majority opinion, *Berghuis v. Thompkins*, 130 S. Ct. 2010 (2010 WL 2160784).
113. Sonia Sotomayor, dissenting opinion, *Berghuis v. Thompkins*, 130 S. Ct. 2010 (2010 WL 2160784).
114. Sotomayor, dissenting opinion, *Berghuis v. Thompkins*, 2010.
115. Sotomayor, dissenting opinion, *Berghuis v. Thompkins*, 2010.
116. Quoted in Adam Phillips, "Justice Sotomayor Returns to Bronx Roots to Cheer Community College Grads," *Voice of America News*, June 5, 2010.

1954
Sonia Sotomayor is born on June 25 in New York, N.Y.

1962
Sonia is diagnosed with type 1 diabetes at the age of eight.

1963
Sonia's father Juan Sotomayor dies suddenly at the age of forty-two.

1968
Sonia is accepted into Cardinal Spellman High School.

1972
Sonia graduates from Spellman High as valedictorian of her class.
She enters Princeton University in September.

1976
Sotomayor graduates from Princeton in June with a BA degree.
She marries high school sweetheart Kevin Noonan in August.
She enters Yale Law School in September.

1979
Sotomayor graduates from Yale in June with a JD degree.
She is hired as an assistant district attorney in New York City in September.

1981–1982
Sotomayor works on Tarzan Burglar murder case.

1983
Sotomayor is divorced from Kevin Noonan.

1984
Sotomayor is hired at the law firm of Pavia & Harcourt, New York City.

1991

U.S. senator Moynihan (D-NY) nominates Sotomayor for district court judgeship on November 29.

1992

Senate confirms Sotomayor for district court judgeship on August 11.

1997

In June President Bill Clinton nominates Sotomayor to fill a vacancy on U.S. Court of Appeals for the Second Circuit.

1998

Senate confirms Sotomayor for appeals court position in October.

2001

In an October 25 speech at Cal–Berkeley School of Law, Sotomayor notes her unique perspective as a "wise Latina woman"; the remark will become controversial during her Supreme Court confirmation proceedings.

2009

May 26: President Barack Obama nominates Sotomayor to the U.S. Supreme Court.

July 13: Senate Judiciary Committee confirmation hearings begin; Sotomayor is questioned about "wise Latina woman" remark in 2001 speech.

July 28: Senate Judiciary Committee approves Sotomayor's nomination.

August 6: Senate confirms Sotomayor's nomination to Supreme Court.

October 5: Sotomayor's first Supreme Court term begins.

2010

On June 4 Bronxdale Houses are renamed the Justice Sonia Sotomayor Houses and Community Center.

adherence: Attachment or loyalty to a person, cause, or idea.

advocacy: Supporting a position or cause.

affirm: Uphold or approve.

arbitration: Settling of differences between two parties by an independent third party.

attorney-client privilege: Protects confidential communications between attorney and client from disclosure.

bias: Prejudice; favoritism.

collective bargaining: Negotiations between a union, representing the employees, and an employer, with regard to salary, benefits, and working conditions.

counterfeit: Fake; an imitation or forgery.

defamatory: Improper injury to a person's reputation by slander or libel.

disparity: Difference.

Establishment Clause: The part of the First Amendment that prohibits the establishment of a national religion by Congress.

fair use doctrine: Allows the reproduction or quotation of a small portion of copyrighted material without permission or authorization.

felony: A serious criminal offense punished by imprisonment.

impartial: Not influenced by bias; fair.

infringe: Violate or disregard someone's rights.

jurisprudence: A code or body of laws.

liable: At risk of; responsible.

litigation: Legal action; proceedings in a lawsuit.

maim: Mangle or damage.

menorah: A nine-branched candlestick used at Hanukkah, a Jewish holiday.

misdemeanor: A criminal offense, less serious than a felony.

parole: Release from prison before the full sentence is served.

plaintiff: A person who brings a lawsuit to court; also called the petitioner.

precedent: A legal decision that serves as the authority or basis for cases that come later.

prosecutor: The person who carries out legal proceedings against someone charged with a crime.

rescind: Cancel; take back; invalidate.

rhetorical: Used for style or effect.

scrutiny: Detailed study or observation.

self-incrimination: To give evidence of one's own guilt or involvement in a crime.

strategic: Thought out; planned.

succinct: Brief; short; concise.

syntax: Patterns and formation of sentences and phrases.

temporary injunction: A court order prohibiting action before legal questions are decided.

tenement: Overcrowded apartment building in poor section of a city.

unanimous: Agreement by all; no objections.

unequivocal: Clear; unmistakable meaning.

Books

Antonia Felix, *Sonia Sotomayor: The True American Dream*. New York: Berkley, 2010. The first adult biography of Sonia Sotomayor to be published.

Lisa Tucker McElroy, *Sonia Sotomayor: First Hispanic U.S. Supreme Court Justice*. Minneapolis: Lerner, 2010. A brief biography written for students.

Tom Thomas, ed., *Sotomayor: Obama's First Supreme Court Nominee*. Seattle: CreateSpace, 2009. Self-published compilation of speeches by Justice Sotomayor and President Obama plus information about the Supreme Court and the Senate.

Periodicals

Richard Lacayo, "Sonia Sotomayor: A Justice Like No Other," *Time*, May 28, 2009. www.time.com/time/print out/0,8816,1901348,00.html.

Evan Thomas, Stuart Taylor Jr., and Brian No, "Meet the Sotomayors," *Newsweek*, July 20, 2009.

Internet Sources

New York Times: "Sotomayor Confirmation Hearing, Day 2" (www.nytimes.com/2009/07/14/us/politics/14confirm-text .html). Transcripts from day 2 of the Sotomayor confirmation hearings.

The Supreme Court of the United States (www.supremecourt .gov). Provides detailed information about the Supreme Court and its cases, rules of the court, and information about the justices.

UCBerkeley News: "A Latina Judge's Voice" (www.berkeley.edu/ news/media/releases/2009/05/26_sotomayor.shtml).Text of the speech in which Sotomayor made her remark about a "wise Latina woman."

United States Senate Committee on the Judiciary (http://judi
ciary.senate.gov). Provides resources for information on nom-
inations and justices from 1879 to the present.

United States Senate Committee on the Judiciary: "Associate
Justice to the Supreme Court—Sonia Sotomayor" (http://
judiciary.senate.gov/nominations/SupremeCourt/Sotomayor
Index.cfm). This section of the Senate Judiciary Committee
website provides access to materials related to the Sotomayor
confirmation, including the Committee questionnaire, support letters, and other information.

Videos

Sonia Sotomayor, "Address at Stamford Middle School to
Bi-lingual Students, Stamford, Connecticut, Fall 2004,"
New York Times Video Library. http://video.nytimes.com/
video/2009/06/10/us/politics/1194840835207/address-at-
stamford-middle-school.html.

"Sonia Sotomayor Confirmation Hearings," C-span video.
www.c-spanvideo.org/program/287672-1.

Sonia Sotomayor, participating panelist, "Facing the 90s as
a Woman Lawyer," Practicing Law Institute, early 1990s,
New York Times Video Library. http://video.nytimes.com/
video/2009/06/10/us/politics/1194840834851/practicing-
law-institute-panelist.html.

Sonia Sotomayor, "Part 2: Interview with Channel 41"
(Spanish-language TV station in New York), October 1994,
New York Times Video Library. http://video.nytimes.com/
video/2009/06/10/us/politics/1194840839964/Part-2-inter
view-with-channel-41.html.

Sonia Sotomayor, "Remarks After Induction to Wall of Fame
at Bronx Community Health Center," September 2007,
New York Times Video Library. http://video.nytimes.com/
video/2009/06/10/us/politics/1194840835085/induction-to-
a-wall-of-fame.html.

Phyllis Raybin Emert is the author of forty-eight books on a wide variety of subjects—from art, animals, and automobiles to unsolved mysteries and women in the Civil War. This is her third title for Lucent Books. Her others are *Art in Glass* and *Pottery*. Phyllis lives in northern New Jersey with her husband Larry and has two grown children, a son-in-law, and two large dogs.